LEADERSHIP
Thirteen studies for individuals or groups

CALVIN MILLER

NAVPRESS
A MINISTRY OF THE NAVIGATORS
P.O. BOX 6000, COLORADO SPRINGS, COLORADO 80934

The Navigators is an international Christian
organization. Jesus Christ gave His followers the
Great Commission to go and make disciples
(Matthew 28:19). The aim of The Navigators is
to help fulfill that commission by multiplying
laborers for Christ in every nation.

NavPress is the publishing ministry of The
Navigators. NavPress publications are tools to
help Christians grow. Although publications
alone cannot make disciples or change lives,
they can help believers learn biblical
discipleship, and apply what they learn to their
lives and ministries.

© 1987 by Calvin Miller
All rights reserved, including translation
Library of Congress Catalog Card Number:
  87-63332
ISBN 08910-91890

Photography: Mark Reis

Unless otherwise identified, all Scripture
quotations in this publication are from the *Holy
Bible: New International Version* (NIV). Copyright ©
1973, 1978, 1984, International Bible Society.
Used by permission of Zondervan Bible
Publishers. Another version quoted is the *King
James Version* (KJV).

Printed in the United States of America

FOR A FREE CATALOG OF
NAVPRESS BOOKS & BIBLE STUDIES,
CALL TOLL FREE 800-366-7788 (USA)
or 800-263-2664 (CANADA)

Contents

Author

Calvin Miller earned a Bachelor of Science degree from Oklahoma Baptist University. He also holds a Master of Divinity degree and a Doctor of Ministry degree from Midwestern Baptist Theological Seminary. He has served as pastor of Westside Church in Omaha, Nebraska, since 1966.

In addition to his pastoral responsibilities, Dr. Miller is the author of nineteen books of popular theology and inspiration, including *The Singer* and *The Song*. His poems and articles have been published in various journals and magazines such as *Christianity Today, Campus Life, Leadership,* and *His*. He serves frequently as an inspirational speaker.

Dr. Miller believes in the primacy of evangelism for the Church in every age. In his ministry, he seeks to be both a contemporary apologist, helping the Church provide answers for a secular society, and an equipper of the contemporary Church for the task of missions and evangelism.

Preface

Leadership is the compass of living. No subject has been more explored in our day than leadership. Management luminaries and other thinkers are constantly addressing the issue. They usually do this in an attempt to tell others how to ride the crest of corporate or political control.

How should we who are Christians view leadership? How should our understanding of leadership differ from that of the secular get-ahead-er?

Every Christian who desires to become a leader must first know how to follow. This book is about King David and you. But I suspect you purchased this book because you are more interested in your leadership skills than David's life. May this book serve both ends.

At the outset, however, let me remind you of an important New Testament principle: If you would be king of all, you must become the servant of all. One of the young deacons of the church I serve paid me the highest compliment when he said, "From your life I have learned that leadership is servanthood." I pray his words are true, for all who are going to be effective Christian leaders must first know how to follow Christ. Jesus warned all would-be entrepreneurs that it does little good to gain the whole world if we lose our souls (Luke 9:25).

This book does not focus directly on Christ, but on David. Still, David of Israel, who lived 1000 years before Christ, models Christian leadership very well. At times in the lives of individuals, corporations, nations, and churches, there is a vacuum of the kind and quality of leadership David's life defines. David's meteoric rise in Israel came at a time when the nation floundered. It needed direction and vision. David, as Jesus suggested, was ready to lead because

7

he had learned how to follow.

You may be called to Christian leadership. If so, may this study challenge you to become all God has called you to be. As we examine the facets of leadership revealed in the life of David—a great yet ordinary man—remember that "great and ordinary" is the usual recipe of leadership. Most great leaders are wonderfully blind to their own significance. As you begin this study, it would be well for you to read 1 Samuel 16 through 2 Samuel 9; the progression of this study will be better understood if you are somewhat familiar with this portion of the life of David as it is chronologically recorded.

—Calvin Miller

Introduction

My pilgrimage from a church planter to the senior pastor of a large and still growing congregation has caused me to have more than a casual interest in the subject of leadership. Leadership is expected of me; perhaps it is even fair to say it is demanded of me. Leadership is imperative if I want to keep the church of which I am pastor on a visionary course. What I have learned by experience these past two decades as a pastor, I have tried to couple with the principles of what I have learned through personal study. The life of David of Israel seems to me to hold a clear outline of the key principles of leadership I wish to present in this study.

As a pastor, I hope the chief points of this study will have a well-tried application for other pastors and church staff leaders. But I have also tried to write this study in a much wider sense to apply to all who are engaged in corporate and industrial leadership as well. Make no mistake: The principles of leadership found in Scripture are applicable in every area of life.

STUDY OBJECTIVES

The objectives of this study are three:

First, I want to let the wisdom of Scripture speak a clear and usable word to the contemporary Christian leader, as well as to anyone who aspires to leadership in the sales or corporate arena. The Bible has sometimes been ignored by the *"Forbes-Magazine-Wall-Street-Journal"* person as a spiritual but pre-modern point of view. It is therefore often seen as beside the point in the right-now world of commerce, entrepreneurship, and technology. My hope is that this study will present the Bible as a contemporary and usable guide in every area of leadership.

9

Second, I want the themes that dominate the current secular business scene to be linked with Scripture. I have tried to be alert to the contemporary management and leadership scene. I have tried to familiarize myself with the works of Harry Levinson, Peter Drucker, James MacGregor Burns, Thomas J. Peters, Warren Bennis, Burt Nanus, and others. I have sought to be alert to the other world of CEO (chief executive officer) literature that I was not generally exposed to in my theological training. While this study is hardly exhaustive, I hope that I have presented the more important principles of leadership.

Third, I hope to define Christian leadership in such a way as to help it escape the haphazard mystique it often acquires. I would like to help you make friends with the most effective concepts of leadership, either in your church or in the corporate world. If this book furnishes you with new tools for leading, or even a few fresh insights in the arena of your leadership, I will be more than compensated.

HOW TO USE THIS STUDY

Don't go too fast! This book should be read slowly over a period of time, allowing ample time to read and study all the Scripture passages in each chapter.

Don't skip the opening quotes for each chapter. I have worked especially hard to ensure that the quotes relate to the chapters at hand. Try to see the correlation as you read through each chapter.

Don't read past any single chapter because you don't see the theme of the chapter as a weakness in your leadership style. Every area of this book has some specific contributions to make to your leadership style.

Do argue with the text when it seems to state leadership principles you disagree with. This book can be wrong, and I hope that it will not be seen as an end-all discussion, but a dialogue of value. In short, let's let our minds meet and reason through each subject.

Do read with a pencil. No book is worth gold unless a little lead marks its consent or denial from page to page. This is a study book. Go ahead, mark it up!

Do realize that a little knowledge is a dangerous thing. If not dangerous, it can be arrogant. Well has the apostle said, "Knowledge destroys." This book is not intended to make you an authority, only to help you get started.

WAYS TO USE THIS STUDY

Alone. If you read this book as a self-study, read it carefully, using your Bible as suggested. It would be best to read one or two other works on leadership at the same time. (You may want to select them from the suggested bibliography.) If you are studying alone, the recommended books will provide a sense of dialogue you might otherwise miss. Be sure to take time for the questions at the end of each chapter. Reading alone might cause you to avoid giving them serious attention and cheat you out of the spirit of dialogue I hope pervades this volume.

For use in small groups (2 to 20 people). When this book is used in small group studies, individual group members should be sure they have well studied the Scripture portion that underlies each discussion. They should, of course, do this before they arrive at the study.

At the start of the class period, someone who reads very well may want to read the significant portions of the chapter to be considered. Then someone else should read much, if not all, of the recommended Scripture.

The rest of the class might then proceed through the study questions with a different group member moderating and leading the discussion of each question.

For use in large groups (20 and up). Large group study leaders may want to encourage class members to:

1. Come to class, having read both the book and the Bible passage to be considered.
2. Listen carefully while the discussion leader presents a formal lesson prepared with the outline I suggest in the book plus augmentation from a great number of other sources. Remember that the best lessons and lectures are still dialogical in tone. Participants in large Bible studies should be mentally "talking with" the leader as they listen.
3. Break into smaller groups whenever possible and get

the material into lively, absorption-reaction discussions.
4. Use a pencil and note pad. In large groups, the textbook should become a workbook full of notes gleaned from both the group leader and small group interactions.

LET'S GO! LET'S LEARN TOGETHER!

1 How Others Perceive a Leader

No human being can exist for long without some sense of his own significance, whether he gets it by shooting a haphazard victim on the street, or by constructive work, or by rebellion, or by psychotic demands in a hospital, or by Walter Mitty fantasies, he must be able to feel this I-count-for-something and be able to live out that felt significance.
Rollo May,
"Power and Innocence"

___

The loss of the leader in some sense or other, the birth of misgivings about him, brings on the outbreak of panic.
Sigmund Freud,
"Group Psychology and the Analysis of the Ego"

___

Why man, he doth bestride the world like a colossus.
William Shakespeare,
"Julius Caesar"

1 Samuel 16:1-13,
18:1-8

It has been well said that "others are the mirrors to yourself." To be an effective leader, you must be perceived as a leader by those you lead. So this book properly begins with a look at yourself.

In chapters sixteen and eighteen of 1 Samuel, how others perceived David is laid out for your examination. Keep these key qualities in the front of your mind as you move from this chapter to the next, in which we shall consider how you perceive yourself.

The importance of the self in the "me" generation has sometimes displaced the importance of others. In an age where selfishness abounds, we must ask, "Does anybody really see a leader? In truth, does anybody see anybody?"

Mike Mason says that in our day there is an overwhelming tendency to treat others as though they are merely extensions of ourselves. Compared with us, therefore, others do not seem to be quite real. "We see them as if through a haze, the haze of our own all-engulfing selfhood."[1] While Mason's rhetoric is hard to deny, it is not altogether true. However high your own self-esteem rises, you do see other people. You observe them and measure all that they are against all that you are. Through such comparison you find out who you are and then take your place in this world. In this gawking society we are all observed, and leaders are scrutinized most of all.

How do leaders appear? In many ways. One thing, however, must be said of all of them: they appear to be leaders! Leadership always declares itself! Leadership never translates as anything less than leadership. I have always disagreed with a poster that once appeared in a Minneapolis barber shop. It presented a picture of Albert Einstein in a last dramatic photograph. The great mathematical genius appears godlike in that photograph with his shock of wild, white hair flying over his keen, deep-set eyes. Yet the caption beneath the poster slurred, "A bad haircut can make anybody look dumb." The comment is both belittling and untrue. Einstein was a leader and can be perceived in no other way, no matter what the poster says.

Friedrich Nietzsche wrote that what most people want

as a model for leadership is a man who is "a strong kind of man, most highly gifted in intellect and will."[2] The gifts that such men possess project as charisma. You may not have taken the time to define charisma, but you know it when you see it.

Charisma, however, may be the least obvious to those who are closest to it. Why is it that in 1 Samuel, Jesse (and indeed, his other sons) seemed to be the last to see David as a potential candidate to be anointed as king? Could it be that David's newness to Samuel caused his charismatic qualities to be so much more apparent than they were to the rest of his family? Had Jesse's family seen David so often that they had really ceased to see him at all?

David was, of course, not the only person in Scripture to whom this happened. Jesus Himself seemed to surprise the good people of His hometown by becoming quite popular. His great charisma as a leader was recognized everywhere, but mostly by those who did not know Him as well as the hometown folks.

There was a very ordinary boy in my hometown who seemed destined to amount to very little. But he surprised us all by becoming a great thoracic surgeon—a true leader in his field. Leaders survive in spite of our vain attempts to contain them in the familiar. They are perceived and their leadership becomes known.

Why is this? John White suggests that leaders have a kind of elitism that cannot be denied. What is this elitism? A winning magnetism. The quality of this magnetism is most attractive in the leader who is not cocky or oversold on his own charisma. He is psychologically secure with no need to "toot his own horn." Even though he seems not to see it, or at least not to dwell on it, his leadership proclaims itself.

We all grant Jesus His singular Godhead, and thus we cannot lump Him together with mere earthly leaders. But I wonder if such self-proclamation is what Jesus might have meant when He said to His critics on Palm Sunday—critics who were trying to shush the crowd—"If these should hold their peace, the stones would immediately cry out" (Luke 19:40, KJV). Make no mistake about it! Who you are and what you are have a way of becoming known in the world.

If this self-proclaiming elitism characterizes your life, will you be able to keep it mixed with enough devotion to God so that others will not see you merely as a leader, but as a Christian leader? You have probably known those who were both elite and godly. The quality of their leadership told you they were elite. The inner Spirit of God told you they were Christians. The mix is unstoppable! Inward substance and outward élan—the Spirit of God and magnetic motivation all in a single life—this is God's recipe for greatness.

What elusive qualities attend such persons?

They are the meek who inherit the earth (Matthew 5:5). They weep and pray in secret, and defy earth and hell in public. They tremble when faced with danger, but die in their tracks sooner than turn back. They are like a shepherd defending his sheep or a mother protecting her young. They sacrifice without grumbling, give without calculating, suffer without groaning.[3]

Christ's followers, with the levers of God and fulcrums of secure selfhood, move the world.

So in 1 Samuel 16-18, the embryonic charisma of the blessed surfaced. Samuel saw it and poured the horn of oil on a boy's head. And what an old prophet perceived as the marks of a leader, the world soon saw and long celebrated.

Questions for Discussion
1. THE PERCEPTION OF LEADERSHIP
Read 1 Samuel 16:1-5.
   a. What do you think the prophet Samuel and Jesse of Bethlehem considered to be the chief attributes of leadership as they gathered Jesse's sons to look for a new king?
   b. What qualities do you like to see in a leader?

2. AVOIDING SUPERFICIALITY
    a. In 1 Samuel 10:23-24, Samuel seemed to pick Saul as king for some obviously superficial reasons. What were those reasons?

    b. Now read 1 Samuel 16:7. Is everyone who looks like a leader really a leader? Why or why not?

    c. What new set of criteria do you think Samuel had in mind when he met with Jesse to anoint the second king of Israel?

    d. Leadership obviously includes some inner qualities that are harder to see. What are some of those hard-to-see qualities?

    e. Which of those qualities are present in your life?

    f. What are your better hard-to-see qualities?

3. THE PECKING ORDER
In 1 Samuel 16:8-9, Jesse seemed to call his sons forth in decreasing order of their stalwart appearance, having begun, of course, with the most impressive and working down to the least impressive. David seemed to be in last place.

    a. Why do you think this was so?

    b. How does a potential leader overcome shortcomings in stature, age, or physical appearance?

    c. When others rate a leader low because he is young, how should that leader reply to the criticism?

    d. First Timothy 4:12 instructs a young leader in how to

maximize his leadership position. What role do you think David's youth played in Jesse's seeming objection to David?

4. ABILITY AND SOCIABILITY

Each of David's psalms shows us that he was a leader who gained outer power by focusing on the inner life.

a. According to 1 Samuel 16:11, would you say David was more of a recluse or a mixer?

b. Which word more accurately characterizes you?

c. How much is the character of leadership forged in aloneness?

d. Are there any real leaders who are unwilling to spend time alone? Explain your answer.

e. As others define leadership, would they—like Jesse—tend to define leaders as extroverts? Or would they be like Samuel and see a leader as emerging from a more aloof lifestyle? Why?

f. Do you think spiritual and secular leadership is more likely to come from a person who is inclined to spend time alone or from one who is always with others?

g. What areas of busy time in your life could you reshape into time alone?

5. THE BEAUTIFUL PEOPLE

First Samuel 16:12 says David's face was beautiful.

a. Do you think, in light of his last-place consideration among the sons of Jesse, this could mean he was not physically handsome?

b. What inner qualities tend to make us appear beautiful?

c. Consider three people you would consider to be beautiful. Are these people physically attractive? Why do they appear beautiful to you?

6. THE SPIRITUAL LIFE OF A LEADER

First Samuel 16:13 says the Spirit of the Lord came upon David; from this point on, he seemed to be marked as a leader of Israel.

a. Do you think the Spirit of God is always obvious in the life of a spiritual leader? If so, in what ways?

b. What qualities of Spirit-led leadership are impossible to find in ordinary leaders?

c. Would the fruit of the Spirit (Galatians 5:22-23) be obvious in every spiritual leader? Which would be the most obvious?

d. Which fruit of the Spirit are most obvious in your life?

7. REFINING VIEWPOINTS

First Samuel 18:5-7 comes after David vanquished Goliath; Saul then saw some qualities of leadership in David.

a. What qualities did Saul see?

b. This seems to be a rather hasty elevation to authority. Can leaders rise too fast? How? Why might this be harmful?

c. Do you think David's early popularity was a help or hindrance to him in his later life? Why?

d. Can people succeed too early in life? What are the possible consequences of premature success?

e. Are you willing to ask God to slow you down until your rate of success leaves room for the lordship of Christ?

NOTES

1. Mike Mason, *The Mystery of Marriage*, Forward by J.I. Packer (Portland: Multnomah Press, 1985), page 37.

2. Friedrich Nietzsche, cited by John White, *Excellence in Leadership* (Downers Grove, Ill.: InterVarsity Press, 1986), page 88.

3. John White, *Excellence in Leadership*, page 89.

2 How a Leader Perceives Himself

The best way to create a good, healthy self-image is to be honest about self-definition. I would like to sing, but I can't.
Steve Brown,
"No More Mr. Nice Guy"

——

[warty bliggens]
considers himself to be
the center of the . . .
universe
the earth exists
to grow toadstools for him
to sit under
the sun to give him light
by day and the moon
and wheeling constellations
to make beautiful
the night for the sake of
warty bliggens
Don Marquis,
"archy and mehitabel"

——

If we do not evaluate our own behavior, or having evaluated it, we do not act to improve our conduct where it is below our standards, we will not fulfill our need to be worthwhile and we will suffer as acutely as when we fail to love or be loved. Morals, standards, values, or right and wrong behavior are all intimately related to the fulfillment of our need for self-worth.
William Glasser,
"Reality Therapy"

1 Samuel 17:19-54

As a leader, your work, like your life, must bear the scrutiny of your own tough evaluation. You will do God no favor if you charge out into the world with no real understanding of who you are. Ignorance about yourself is a self-imposed limitation that will keep much of your leadership potential from developing.

Did David understand who he was? Let's see how much he really knew about who he was and what God expected of him.

In the passage on which this chapter is focused, David seems to have conquered the inner giant of self-doubt as he battles his formidable outer foe, Goliath. The toughness of an outer foe, however, may be a piece of cake in comparison to our inner foe. The reason many potential leaders never develop has little to do with the toughness of their outer foes. Outer foes and tough circumstances are roughly the same for all. The giants on the inside are the real problems.

Abraham Maslow, in his *Toward a Psychology of Being*, concludes that persons of low self-esteem are not only more frenzied in their lifestyles, but are also less imaginative. They are, therefore, far less likely to become successful leaders than persons who have better learned to manage the tough inner foe of self.[1]

David's competence does not come from a trumped-up, latent egoism. His dependence is upon God. Still, you must be careful as you balance self-denial and self-esteem in your life; you must not pretend that faith in God means automatic self-esteem. Robert Schuller has repeatedly pointed out that as a group, evangelical Christians consistently rate lowest in self-esteem polls. Why? Perhaps because of certain post-reformation (largely Calvinist) views of the depravity of man. Perhaps you were taught as a child to see yourself as loathsome to your Maker. If you see yourself as loathsome to God, you can then become loathsome to yourself. Jean-Paul Sartre in *The Flies* has a man crying out, "I stink! Oh, how I stink! I am a mass of rottenness. . . . I have sinned a thousand times . . . and I reek to heaven!"[2]

For 400 years we evangelicals have been telling ourselves that we are totally depraved. For forty decades we have put ourselves so far down that we find it hard to really see the God-given good in our lives. We must never excuse man's fallen condition. Human willfulness is the reason for the cross of Christ. Even though we are fallen, however, we are also stamped with the *imago dei* (the image of God) and can legitimately celebrate the good things that are part of us. This is especially true of those who have made Christ Lord of their lives.

We often speak of the imperative self-esteem. Certainly self-esteem is imperative in the life of every really secure leader. But what is self-esteem? Stanley Coopersmith defines self-esteem as "the evaluation which the individual makes and customarily maintains with regard to himself: it expresses an attitude of approval or disapproval, and indicates the extent to which the individual believes himself to be capable, significant, successful, and worthy."[3] For the real leader, this evaluation is not only important, it is essential.

In a *Wall Street Journal* article, the inference is made that people of low self-esteem can manage but can never lead. One thing is sure: leadership and management often fall into widely separate categories. The article goes on to say that no one is really eager to be managed, while the entire world is hungry to be led. Consider the powerful truth of these words:

> If you want to
> manage somebody,
> manage yourself.
> Do that well
> and you'll
> be ready to
> stop managing.
> And start leading.[4]

This article was subtitled, "Let's Get Rid of Management." So often, managers only manage what leaders have brought into being. This book is not a call to manage, but a call to lead.

In the Bible study at hand, you are examining the life

of a leader who found that the will of God was the only adequate mirror to his self-image. Once David found out what God wanted with him, the direction of his leadership was decided. It is not such a fearsome thing to lead once you see your leadership as a part of God's overall plan for His world.

When I was a boy, I was fascinated by the railroad tracks that passed my home. My mother told me there were engineers that drove trains more than 200 miles per day.

"It must be hard to drive trains such long distances," I said to her.

"No. He must only pull a few levers; the rest of his journey is up to the rails." She put my mind at rest.

Great Christian leaders ride the rails of obedience. They are responsible for the whole distance, but not the direction. Direction is the treasure that is given to Christian men or women who lead.

David set the throttle of his life to serve the pure pleasure of God. The rails carried him to the pinnacle of human history. Seek the rails that are labeled "the pleasure of God." Pray always that you stay on track. Then you will keep in touch with meaning—and rest in this: Meaning and failure do not keep company in life. Neither do low self-esteem and pleasing God. Seeing and accepting your God-given strengths will make you usable to the God who gave them to you.

Questions for Discussion
1. THE HARD WORK OF SELF-ANALYSIS
In 1 Samuel 17:26, it is clear that David does not perceive his task in terms of his own strength. His task is formidable. His own resources are limited.
   a. What you accomplish in the power of God marks you as a spiritual leader. How should you label what you accomplish in your own name?
   b. How often do you forget to deal with your circumstances in terms of power greater than your own?
   c. How could memorizing scriptures like Romans 12:3-5 or Philippians 4:13 encourage you to see yourself honestly in terms of your strengths and weaknesses?

   d. Make a list of your strengths and weaknesses and see
     how the list relates to your leadership potential.

2. GETTING GOD INVOLVED IN SELF-STUDY
In 1 Samuel 17:28, David is demoralized by Eliab's criticism that he is more a shepherd than a soldier.

   a. A leader needs a good measure of self-confidence,
     but how do you hold on to it in the face of demoralizing criticism from family or close friends?

   b. How can relying on God give you a view of your own
     strength that the criticisms of even well-meaning friends cannot chip away?

   c. David no doubt had some compelling encounter with
     God. How does your own encounter with God change your view of yourself?

   d. Which of your glaring weaknesses have been overcome by encountering God?

   e. How can you as a potential leader develop a strong
     view of yourself that can endure criticism without becoming arrogant?

3. LETTING YOUR PAST GUIDE YOUR FUTURE

In 1 Samuel 17:34-36, David views his ability to handle future problems in light of his successful past performance.

a. In what ways should you lean on past performances to give you future confidence?

b. Think of a problem you had during this last month: Did you confront this problem with a strong self-perception?

c. Does the way you see God involved in your past successes indicate how you are likely to see Him involved in your future confrontations? Explain your answer.

d. Write down three outstanding qualities of leadership you see in your life. In what ways have you already used these qualities to handle tough circumstances?

4. LEADERSHIP AND TRADITIONAL THINKING

In 1 Samuel 17:38-39, David is encouraged to succeed in a traditional way, yet he refuses the customary battle attire.

a. Are leaders usually traditional thinkers? In what ways are they traditional or not traditional?

b. David knows how he must fight and refuses Saul's armor. What does his statement, "I have not proved them," really mean?

c. Others saw David's plan for success as suicidal. When are we wise to listen to the advice of others?

d. What David did was a creative approach to giant-killing. David was living under the continual confi-

dence of the leadership of God's Spirit (1 Samuel 16:13). Is God's Spirit usually more creative or traditional in His leadership?
   e. Does David's self-understanding come totally from his past experience with success? How much do you think comes from his quiet introspection?
   f. How can you arrive at this kind of self-understanding?

5. DEALING WITH CRITICISM
First Samuel 17:42-43 gives a good picture of David's self-confidence surviving under the attack of an enemy.
   a. Do you think Eliab's criticism (1 Samuel 17:28) was harder to bear than Goliath's? If so, why? If not, why not?
   b. How would you maintain a leader's confidence in the face of criticism?
   c. What sort of criticism debilitates you most?

6. THE ISSUE OF REPUTATION

In 1 Samuel 17:46-47, David demonstrates that a spiritual leader evaluates what his success will mean in terms of the reputation of God.

a. How can your self-understanding be used in a positive way as a witness to others?

b. Are great Christian leaders always aware of how their careers make God look good in the eyes of others? Explain your answer.

7. THE PARALYSIS OF ANALYSIS

In 1 Samuel 17:53-54, after a great deal of challenge and introspection, David incites a whole army to action.

a. When is self-analysis self-defeating?

b. How much time did David spend contemplating Goliath and his own strength?

c. How often do you allow self-examination to become a substitute for real action?

NOTES
1. Abraham H. Maslow, *Toward a Psychology of Being* (New York: Van Nostrand Reinhold, 1968).
2. Jean-Paul Sartre, *No Exit and Three Other Plays* (New York: Random House [Vintage Books], 1948), page 77.
3. Stanley Coopersmith, *The Antecedents of Self-Esteem* (San Francisco: Freeman, 1967), pages 4-5.
4. A message as published in the *Wall Street Journal* by United Technologies Corporation, Hartford, Connecticut, cited in Warren Bennis & Burt Nanus, *Leaders: The Strategies for Taking Charge* (New York: Harper & Row, 1985), page 22.

3 Networking and the Special Friends of a Leader

Relations with peers are enormously difficult for the person aspiring to supreme leadership.
James MacGregor Burns,
"Leadership"

———

I hope when I die there will be at least five of my friends who will be able to sit through my funeral without looking at their watches.
The leader of a large Christian organization
to R. C. Sproul

———

We sip the foam of many lives.
Ralph Waldo Emerson

1 Samuel 18:1-4,
20:1-5,8,20-22

A great leader is never a "Lone Ranger." Every leader knows that his or her leadership has been earned by a great many people who are a part of his or her "network." Many current motivators use the word *network* to speak of the matrix of relationships that provide the people resources for success. You may have heard it said that behind a great man is a great woman who contributes to all her husband becomes. And behind a dynamic woman is often the supporting confidence and help of family and friends. In a similar way, behind every great leader there are a great many special friends. Their allegiance to the leader is foundational to all he or she achieves. If you should become a great leader, never forget the people who have made your leadership possible.

In the passages listed above, David and Jonathan not only became friends, but their friendship pledged itself in marvelous allegiance. Without Jonathan, David might have been killed by the king's assassins. Had that happened, Israel's great light would have been extinguished.

To have quality in your life, you must have loyal friends; these friends compose the network out of which (and upon which) your leadership can reach for excellence. In many ways, however, the word *network* implies that friends are only things to be used rather than persons to be served. No view of friendship could be more debilitating or unChristian. Remember, Jesus said to His disciples, "I no longer call you servants. . . . Instead, I have called you friends" (John 15:15, NIV). Did Jesus call us friends because He conceived us to be a part of some malleable network He could shape for His own selfish ends? Certainly not! Since He is our model, we must never view our network as something to be manipulated for our interests alone.

Judy Viorst suggests that there are six categories of friends: 1) convenience friends, 2) special-interest friends, 3) historical friends, 4) crossroads friends, 5) cross-generational friends, and 6) close friends.[1] These categories are rather self-explanatory, and David must have had friends in all six categories.

What is most significant about David's friendship with

God? David determined that this friendship would be a real priority in his life. We evangelicals often sing, "What a friend we have in Jesus," and by this I presume we are considering our friendship with God to be a category six friendship—close friends. Emilie Griffin makes a dynamic statement concerning our friendship with God:

> This friendship is friendship with God and with others because of God. It is a friendship not of the flesh, but of adoption, a spiritual bond that echoes Shakespeare's words:
>
> > Those friends thou hast, and their adoption tried,
> > Grapple them to thy soul with hoops of steel.
>
> But the grappling is done not by us, but by grace.[2]

The very word *election* implies that God did the first choosing to be friends with us. Our choosing was important, but it came later.

Still, as a potential leader you must have important friends in category six: friends who are indispensable to your success. It is touching that Lee Iacocca cited his barber as one of his close friends during his time of great stress. Any leader has friends who often do not measure up to the standards of social, political, or economic leadership, but who serve behind the scenes in critical ways.

Your friendship with God is rooted in a paradox. You reach to God as you seek to maintain a critical balance—the balance between intimacy and awe. Sometimes, out of great respect, you may sing, "Praise, my soul, the King of Heaven." At other times you will sing, "What a Friend I have in Jesus." Which song expresses your friendship with God? Both, of course! In the balance between awe and intimacy, you celebrate a Friend whose power to help you is as great as His personal interest in your life.

In the passage we are about to study, David and Jonathan affirm their love for each other. In a sexually ambiguous world, evangelicals have steered away from all talk of a love "surpassing the love of women" (2 Samuel 1:26). Still, here at the onset of David's reign, we need to see how much he owed Jonathan and his other friends. The others never reached David's pinnacle of historical importance, but without them David's place in history could never have come to be.

Questions for Discussion
1. THE CHEMISTRY OF FRIENDSHIP (1 Samuel 18:1)
In this passage the word *knit* (as used in the *King James Version*) is a graphic way to describe friendship. The knitting metaphor can be seen two ways. *Knitting* suggests an interweaving of threads to form a whole fabric. *Knitting* also means the process of mending broken, human limbs in which fractured or fragmented bones grow slowly together in a strong, physical weld.
   a. In what ways do these metaphors speak of loyalty and oneness in relationship?
   b. In this passage there is an "automaticness" in the friendship of David and Jonathan. We sometimes call this "chemistry." The good feeling you have as you think of your friends is the language of chemistry. You can't always analyze logically what makes you choose some people as your friends and deny others, but you can see that it is somewhat intuitive. Is chemistry a reliable way to decide who will be your friends and who will not? Explain your answer.
   c. We often say friendship is "all in the vibes." Should we be more rational about it? Can we be?
   d. Do you think David and Jonathan had a stable relationship because they liked each other (and that's how we describe the chemistry of friendship) or because they were both involved in national affairs?

2. THE "SHIRT-OFF-MY-BACK" SYNDROME
(1 Samuel 18:3-4)
We often hear the cliché "shirt off my back."
a. In what way does this cliché describe the event in this passage?
b. Remembering that David was a shepherd and Jonathan a prince, how does this story indicate that Jonathan saw the coming of greatness in David?
c. In terms of leadership, is the chemistry of first relationships a good thing for a leader to trust in later crises?
d. David was primarily a poet and Jonathan a warrior. Consider some aspects of personality that they held in common. Do great leaders have to have everything in common with their most loyal supporters?
e. How much affirmation should friends give each other verbally? Read 2 Samuel 1:26.
f. What do you think David meant when he celebrated the "love that surpassed the love of women"?
g. Much of the love that expresses itself in support of a leader is "same-sex" love. Are most leaders better able to affirm those of the same sex who are basic to their networks than those of the opposite sex? Why or why not?

3. THE AFFIRMATION OF LEADERSHIP
(1 Samuel 20:4)
Leaders and followers must be able to compliment and affirm one another.

a. How have leaders that you admire been able to do this?

b. In what great leaders did you observe a deficiency of that quality?

c. Can you think of a position in which you have been a subordinate, but were encouraged by a leader who had a great deal of understanding?

4. LEADERS AREN'T POSSESSIVE WITH THEIR FRIENDS (1 Samuel 20:5)

Jonathan still ate with his father. He surely must have been torn between supporting David and being loyal to his own father, his best friend's enemy.

One expert in church-staff relationships says that many church staffs have serious problems because Christians become possessive with friends.

a. How do you think a great leader grants wideness to his networking group in allowing them to have friends other than himself?

b. How do career promotions isolate leaders and make them feel lonely? Does it have to be "lonely at the top" for all leaders?

c. All through his long struggle with King Saul, David overcame his need to get even. What kinds of inner tension did David bring on himself by caring so much for Jonathan that he refused to injure Jonathan's father—his own worst enemy? (See 1 Samuel 24:1-7.)

5. LOYALTY OATHS (1 Samuel 20:8)
David put his life in the hands of Jonathan.
a. Why did he see this as necessary?
b. Do loyalty oaths usually set friendship free, or do they constrict it?
c. Do you think the promise David made in this verse was one that he lived out throughout his life?
d. Should trust be verbalized often? Why or why not?

NOTES
1. Judith Viorst, *Necessary Losses* (New York: Simon & Schuster, 1986), pages 179-180.
2. Emilie Griffin, *Clinging* (San Francisco: Harper & Row, 1984), page 43, citing Shakespeare, *Hamlet*, act I, scene iii, line 62.

4 Vision

If your eye be single, your whole body will be full of light.
Jesus of Nazareth,
"The Sermon on the Mount"

Did you know that studies have shown it is almost impossible to give a dog an ulcer? Do you know why? Because dogs hardly ever try to be anything but a dog.
Steve Brown,
"No More Mr. Nice Guy"

For the man who cannot wonder,
is but a pair of spectacles behind which there is no eye.
Thomas Carlyle

2 Samuel 5:1-10 The entire industrialized complex that *is* America huddles around the word *vision*. Vision is a word to drop if you want immediate attention from managers and planners. Literally thousands of visioning conferences are sponsored by the CEOs of America's important thriving corporations. But what does the word *vision* literally mean? Proverbs 29:18 reads, "Where there is no vision the people perish!" Most contemporary CEOs would agree with this verse. Dynamic leadership is always fired by vision.

Let us begin by trying to understand the nature of vision in general. Karl Jaspers was an existential philosopher who taught that all giving, to be meaningful, had to touch some "final experience." This authenticating "final experience" comes when a person reaches an "axial point." This "axial point" is a crisis that brings us a new vision that redefines our lives.

Does *vision* seem too grand a word to apply to your own life or career? How do you get vision? Where does vision come from?

Often, vision is the result of some tearing, ripping circumstance by which you have come to an end of your own ability to make life work. But don't deplore such times! In the neurotic stress of such times you may achieve a breakthrough. This breakthrough may be an exhilarating insight, once symbolized by the Ford Motor Company with the better-idea light bulb. It may really be a laser of hope that snaps on in your gray existence and illuminates some new direction—a clear glory you had not been able to see before the pain came. In short, it may be the conveyance to Jaspers's axial point. Such desperation often prefaces life-changing vision.

One thing is for sure: without the axial point and its welcome new vision, life for most of us is mundane. Visionless living provides no real *raison d'etre* (reason to be). Vision is the only escape from aimlessness: "After his conversion to Marxism in 1963, [playwright Peter] Weiss stated that the effect of aimlessness in the West was to destroy at the root all cultural and creative activity."[1]

Vision is as important to nations as it is to individuals. A little later in our study we will further examine Proverbs 29:18, which says that without vision whole cultures can perish.

You need to understand three things about the nature of vision: first, its inherent power; second, where it comes from; and finally, how you hold on to it.

First, consider the inherent power of vision in your life. Its dynamic is the enthusiasm it infuses. The enthusiasm inspired by vision results in some kind of life product. Feelings of productivity increase your feelings of self-esteem. This self-esteem causes a healthy celebration of your usefulness to God and your world. A former NCR employee described vision this way: "Genius is intensity. The salesman who surges with enthusiasm, though it is excessive, is superior to the one who has no passion. I would prefer to calm down a geyser than start with a mudhole."[2]

The power of enthusiasm is the energy that drives every successful idea. And enthusiasm has its taproot in the fertile soil of vision. We will see shortly how all of this operated in the life of David of Israel.

But where does vision come from? Ralph Neighbour, Jr., says that the seven first words of the Church are, "I can do all things through Christ."[3] Surely Christ is the font of our best imagination and vision. The finest visions that can possess a man come directly from God through Christ.

But I must sound this word of warning. God does not shout His best vision through hassled Christian living. It is in quiet that He gives the most delivering visions of life. Psychologist Nathaniel Branden wrote:

> Innovators and creators are persons who can to a higher degree than average accept the condition of aloneness. They are more willing to follow their own vision even when it takes them far from the mainland of the human community.[4]

Alan Loy McGinnis also reminds us that "Jesus' life was checkered with solitude."[5]

The final essential aspect of vision that you must understand is how to hold onto it. Holding onto a redeeming vision through all kinds of trials can be hard. New visions burn brighter than old ones. In the press of your days and years, old dreams can lose their fire and hence the enthusiasm they once supplied. A wealthy American immigrant sadly testified, "I heard that in America there was a pot of gold at the end of the rainbow. I found the gold but, young man, I lost the rainbow." Clinging to rainbows can be your most arduous task.

Perhaps it needs to be said that your visions will serve you best not when you are their keepers, but when they are yours. Your visions will be far more productive when they possess you. So the real issue is not how do you hold your visions, but how your visions keep you.

I want to suggest two ingredients for the recipe of vision-keeping. Number one is an adequate quiet time. When you are quiet at the altar of your own trust, your vision will hold its place in your life. Visions rebuild themselves in quietness, not in the hurry and noise of life.

A second ingredient of vision-keeping is rehearsal. Constantly, you must rehearse your dreams. It is not enough to have rehearsed them in the past. They must be a part of every day, or soon they will not keep faith with any day.

Now let us examine the life of David of Israel and see what we can learn from his vision that may supply life to your own.

Vision is a dream inebriated by imagination. David was a man of vision and in 2 Samuel 5:1-10 he takes a giant step in favor of a powerful symbol—Zion—Jerusalem. The city—even the citadel—came to be idealized as Zion, the completed city of God. The late Martin Luther King once cried before a massive audience in Washington, D.C., "I have a dream!"

Dreams are characteristic of leaders. David, too, had a dream—a city for the center of God's presence in the world. Such visions fuel leadership—no great leadership ever exists without the power of vision.

Vision serves leadership in five ways.

Questions for Discussion
1. VISION UNITES (2 Samuel 5:1)

The nation that was fragmented after the death of Saul and the civil struggles of Saul's princes left the new monarchy sadly divided. In division they were weak and thus opted for national unity by asking David to be king. David was a new visionary who was able to give them a feeling of oneness again.

a. Describe a time when a badly divided organization suddenly received a new, driving vision. How did it happen? What was the result?

b. Is 2 Samuel 5:2 a criticism of Saul or a plea for a new vision? Explain your answer.

c. In what ways are the words *purpose* and *calling* synonymous with the idea of vision?

d. Do you think the confused leaders of the nation saw David's vision as something that would be costly to them? If so, in what way?

e. Do great visions usually have high price tags?

f. What kinds of price tags come with the visions of God?

g. Have you ever been in a place where you have had to weigh the relative cost of God's vision for your life as opposed to more ordinary human dreams? What was that experience like?

**2. VISION PROVIDES A CENTER FOR LEADERSHIP
(2 Samuel 5:5)**
David began his reign in the south, in Hebron, a city a
long distance from the center of the nation. David's
vision was to rule a unified Israel with his throne in the
middle of the nation. After seven years at Hebron, he
moved his throne of government to Jerusalem.

a. A center for leadership is a focus that often comes
   through the vision of a great leader. Do you agree that
   the center of focus in David's life was the will of God?

b. Do you agree that the central purpose of God has a
   way of prioritizing secondary aspects of God's plans
   for your life? Why or why not?

c. Have you isolated what you believe is God's central
   calling and purpose in your life? What is it?

d. Do you think the strength of David's driving dream
   was related to the quickness with which he conquered
   Jerusalem? Why do you think this?

e. What evidences are there that David's driving vision
   made him impatient?

f. What is the relationship between strength of leadership and impatience?

3. VISION DOMINATES ALL INNER CONVERSATION (2 Samuel 5:6)

All of us indulge in inner conversation that is "off limits" to everyone but ourselves. Throughout our lives this inner conversation presides over our vision and pushes us to our destiny.

a. Is it possible that the Jebusites (who lived in the walled city of Jebus, that David later named Jerusalem) gave David a challenge during his seven years at Hebron? Explain your answer.

b. David's inner conversation seemed to be dominated by one thought: "Someday I will rule all this land from the walled city of Jebus." Like David, you, too, can tell where you're headed by what you think about. What thoughts dominate the inner conversation of your mind?

c. How do you think the phrase, "As a man thinketh . . . so is he" (Proverbs 23:7) relates to the whole matter of inner conversation and vision?

d. What is the difference between a one-track mind and single-mindedness?

e. Do dominating life visions tend to produce single-minded people?

f. Can we justify having a one-track mind even if the rails are made straight for one destiny with the purpose of God?

g. A fanatic is often defined as anyone who can't change his mind and won't change the subject. Are fanatics ever visionary? Why or why not?

h. How were David's difficulties made easier to overcome by his singleness of vision?

i. Do you consider yourself to be goal-oriented? In what ways?

j. Are goal-oriented people the same thing as visionaries? Why or why not?

k. Have you isolated your own vision? What is it?

l. Do you think some people "cop out" in leadership roles by saying they are "waiting for the Lord to lead"? How can you recognize that in yourself or someone else?

m. Does every aspect of your vision need to be clearly in mind before you begin to move toward your goal? Why or why not?

4. VISION IS THE SYMBOL THAT INSPIRES
(2 Samuel 5:7)

David accepted the challenge of the Jebusites, and soon reigned in Jerusalem. Jerusalem—city of Peace, the citadel, the utopian city of God, Zion—all these names for his city were synonyms of David's achievement.

a. Think of various kinds of symbols (flags, statues, ideas) and the strength of their inspiration. Which of these symbols marked David's conquest of Jerusalem?

b. What symbols motivate you? Prioritize them, beginning with the strongest symbol.

c. Make a list of five great, contemporary, national leaders: What were their driving dreams?

d. How would you prioritize David's dreams: a central

throne, a citadel, building the Temple, and subduing the surrounding city-states?
e. What things would you like to accomplish in the course of your life? Take time to prioritize them.

5. VISIONS INSPIRE GREATNESS (2 Samuel 5:10)
David's arrival in the citadel of Jerusalem was the realization of years of dreaming.
a. Do you think verse 10 is the end goal of every leader whose life and inner conversation are driven by a great vision?
b. Verse 10 says David grew in greatness. Is personal growth an automatic corollary of vision? Why or why not?
c. How do we bridge the gap between the achievement of our goals and the current state of our dreams?
d. Write down the steps in your own life between Hebron and Jerusalem (between where you are now and where you want to be). Becoming a leader means choosing to serve your life vision and "concretizing" it. One way to "concretize" your vision is to write it down. Let 2 Samuel 5:10 motivate you to do this important activity.

NOTES
1. Klaus Bockmuehl, *The Challenge of Marxism* (Downers Grove, Ill.: InterVarsity Press, 1980), page 39.
2. Alan Loy McGinnis, *Bringing Out the Best in People* (Minneapolis: Augsburg Publishing House, 1985), page 169.
3. Ralph W. Neighbour, Jr., *The Seven Last Words of the Church* (Nashville: Broadman Press, 1979), page 19.
4. Nathaniel Branden, *The Psychology of Romantic Love* (Los Angeles: J.P. Tarcher, 1980), page 61.
5. McGinnis, *Bringing Out the Best in People*, page 163.

5 | Decision: The Key to Leadership

It ain't nothin' 'til I call it.
An American umpire

—

Two roads diverged in a wood, and I—
I took the one less traveled by,
And that has made all the difference.
Robert Frost,
"The Road Not Taken"

—

Leaders, whatever their professions of harmony, do not
shun conflict; they confront it, exploit it, ultimately
embody it.
James MacGregor Burns,
"Leadership"

2 Samuel 6:1-15,
7:1-13

Leaders are decision makers. Most of us quail before the lonely work of making decisions. We need a pier in the ocean of alternatives—solid footing on which to say yes or no. Is there a more certain way to act in times of uncertainty?

Throughout Israel's wilderness sojourn, the Ark of the Covenant was located in the Tabernacle and was the central altarpiece of the Exodus experience. The tents, shanties, and portable lean-tos of the rest of Israel were gathered around the Ark. Thus it, and the God who hovered above the mercy seat, were central in Israel's uncertain time (forty years) of sojourn.

In this passage we see that Israel has a proud new capital, Jerusalem, which means "city of peace." But David realized it would become a city of turmoil if God did not direct the nation from its very center. Since the Ark of the Covenant symbolized God's presence on earth, it needed to be within the walls of Jerusalem. Then every decision could be made in the security that God was not peripheral to what was going on.

Like all great leaders, David was decisive. For him, all decision making began and ended with God. His need to move the Ark into Jerusalem was based on his conviction that great leaders make decisions after they have consulted with God. So David's decision to bring the Ark to Jerusalem became the pier decision on which he based the smaller decisions of his monarchy.

Every leader must know how to recognize and make pier decisions. Like David, you need to see that pier decisions are those that place God at the center of things. For the Christian, the first pier decision is to admit Christ into one's life to take His rightful place of lordship. Evangelicals generally refer to this pier decision as "making a decision for Christ." You very likely have already made such a decision.

Yet the statement, "make a decision for Christ" is not totally honest. When you admit Christ to His rightful place of lordship, you are really making a decision for yourself as much as for Christ. So the decision is a pier decision in every way. Figuratively, you are deciding to bring the "Ark"—the consultation of God—into critical influence in your decision-making process.

For the real leader, pier decisions serve in four ways: 1) they divide life into manageable segments, 2) they create new beginnings, 3) they contribute to a strong sense of self, and 4) they force us into lifelong participation with God that leads to meaningful living.

Let us consider how decisions divide life into manageable segments. David never forgot the day he brought the Ark of the Covenant into the Holy City. It became for him the milestone of his long, productive reign. In a similar way, coming to Christ for the first time marks such a dividing of life. All that was before that decision is loss. All that comes after that decision is redemption.

Marriage proposals and military enlistments are other decisions that mark the great divisions of life. By merely saying, "I do," we divide twenty years of singleness from fifty years of marriage. In a similar way, by saying, "Lord, I believe," we change from years of lostness to meaningful years of Christ-directed living.

A second way decisions serve is by creating new beginnings. Your decisions, right or wrong, create places for you to start again. Certainly you have sometimes found life to be mundane or boring. In such drudgerous circumstances, a fresh start is always welcome. A good, firm decision can provide a starting place at which to choose a new direction.

One of the best ways decisions serve is to provide a strong sense of self. They do this by summoning, from your innermost self, the ego force necessary to make decisions. Certainly David must have had criticism of his administration—perhaps of his decision to bring the Ark into the Holy City. But he acted in the face of criticism and became a stronger person after having made the decision. When you exercise personal courage, you will always become stronger.

Decisions also serve your sense of self by reminding you that you are responsible for your own life and fortune. Decisive lifestyles teach that to a large part you make yourself. Brick by brick, as a mason builds a tower, you do indeed make yourself. The bricks that compose the tower of your life are the single decisions that compose a collective destiny.

Finally, decisions create a sense of self by forcing you into the cauldrons of refining loneliness. Others may help you clarify decisions, but you must decide alone. Obadiah Milton Conover wrote:

> Alone I walk the peopled city
>   Where each seems happy with his own;
> O friends, I ask not for your pity—
>   I walk alone.[1]

Yet the loneliness of decision making is not a desolate aloneness, but a reaching aloneness. Decisions make you a partner with God. The insecurity of making decisions clearly shows that in order to be right, it is necessary to be on God's side.

You are probably aware that about fifty percent of all decisions you make will be wrong. God can make a difference in lowering this dreadful percentage. John Maxwell wrote that great decisions are often as much a matter of timing as event:

> The wrong decision at the wrong time = disaster.
> The wrong decision at the right time = mistake.
> The right decision at the wrong time = unacceptance.
> The right decision at the right time = success.[2]

As you examine the life of David, you will unfold the principles of decision making. Learn from them. Seek your own maturity in leadership by becoming responsibly decisive.

Questions for Discussion
1. GOOD DECISION MAKERS WANT GOD NEAR
AT HAND
The Ark was the central altar of a portable shrine called the Tabernacle. The Tabernacle was really a portable cathedral made of rich hangings and costly gold and brazen fixtures. The Tabernacle and the Ark had been built by divine order during Israel's wilderness sojourn

that lasted for 40 years. After David occupied Jerusalem
(2 Samuel 6:2), the Ark at last came to dwell within the
security of a walled fortress.

a. Does David appear to be a leader who would consult
God before every decision? What elements in the
young king's life indicate that he customarily sought
God's leadership?

b. Psalm 51 (which we will consider more fully in chapter nine) indicates that David, in a time of remorse
over sin, consulted God. What words in verses 10-12
(printed below), make us believe that David might
have prayed before the Ark of the Covenant?

> Create in me a pure heart, O God,
>   and renew a steadfast spirit within me.
> Do not cast me from your presence
>   or take your Holy Spirit from me,
> Restore to me the joy of your salvation
>   and grant me a willing spirit, to sustain me.
>
> (Psalm 51:10-12)

c. Have you been forced on occasion to make decisions
when you felt God was far away? Describe one
experience.

d. James 4:8 challenges us to draw near to God, and
counsels us to cleanse our minds. How can you draw
near to God in prayer? How do you cleanse your mind
of "busyness"?

2. GOOD DECISION MAKING RESPECTS THE POWER OF GOD

Decisions gain ethical correctness when we understand God's great power. The burden of being near God lies in the immensity of His power. In 2 Samuel 6:6-7, Uzzah was destroyed not because he was bad, but because he touched the Ark. (The Ark was designed to be carried with rings and rods so no human hand would ever have to touch it.)

a. Ecclesiastes 12:13 instructs us to "fear God and keep his commandments." Do you think leaders should approach God with fear, love, or a combination of the two? Cite a practical example to illustrate your answer.

b. Hebrews 12:29 says God is a consuming fire. What do you think a verse like this means in terms of the divine respect we should give God?

c. Certainly Uzzah's misfortune after touching the Ark should keep us from claiming too flippantly that we have made easy decisions that God would honor. What steps should you take to ensure that you have earnestly inquired of God concerning His direction?

3. GOOD LEADERSHIP DECIDES IN AN ATMOSPHERE OF JOY IN WORSHIP

Second Samuel 6:14-15 describes David as dancing "before the Lord with all his might" when Israel brought the Ark into the city.

a. Although David's sense of praise may seem excessive to us (it certainly seemed excessive to his wife—

2 Samuel 6:20), what does his joy in worship teach
about the importance of praise in a leader's life?
b. Can you name some important government officials
who attend church?
c. How do you feel about those in positions of leadership who see no need to attend worship services?
d. David seemed ecstatic as he rejoiced over the coming
of the Ark. Do you feel that worship should be held in
check or given free expression?
e. What effect does praise have on decision-making?
f. Should every leader seek to honor God with regular
praise times? How regular?

4. GOOD LEADERSHIP DECIDES FOR GOD BEFORE IT DECIDES IN FAVOR OF ONE'S SELF

It is a mark of spiritual maturity to consider how our
decisions will be good for God before we contemplate
the benefit they will bring to us. David felt badly because
he had a permanent house while the Ark did not (2
Samuel 7:2). He demonstrated great spiritual sensitivity
in making the decision to bring the Ark to Jerusalem.
How can you develop such a heart for God so that you
think of God's ends before you contemplate your own?

5. GOOD LEADERSHIP MAKES DECISIONS TO POSTPONE DECISIONS

Decisiveness does not mean we always decide to do something. In 2 Samuel 7:10-12 David decided to do nothing, a decision that was approved by God.

a. Describe a time in your life when you decided not to make a decision because you lacked the proper information to make a good decision.

b. Sometimes God wants us to entrust the future to Him: David had to ask, "Does what I want to do have to be done now?" Why was it better for David to decide to let Solomon build the Temple?

c. How may time measure the quality of your decisions?

d. Describe a time in your life when you ran ahead of God with a decision.

6. TEAM PLAYING WITH THE FUTURE

Every leader knows the value of team playing, but in 2 Samuel 7:13 the subject is the issue of team playing with the future. The way a leader's work survives him, or is fulfilled, may well depend upon those to whom he commits his vision. Here, Solomon will obviously complete the dream of David.

a. Construction of the Rheims Cathedral was handed down from one generation to the next for hundreds of years. Who can you think of who dreamed dreams that required them to surrender their work to those who would come after them? Would the impatience of most leaders permit this?

b. When Paul tells Timothy to entrust his teachings to reliable men (2 Timothy 2:2), he seems to indicate that even the existence of straight thinking from one generation to the next is a matter of trusting those who survive us. How much is all of Christian tradition a team effort?

c. Does a parent demonstrate trusting leadership when he or she passes on the truth of Christianity to his or her children? Explain your answer.

d. Do you think David ever shared his uncompleted temple dream with Prince Solomon? List any scriptural evidences that Solomon took his father's charge seriously.

NOTES

1. Obadiah Milton Conover, *Bartlett's Familiar Quotations* (Boston: Little, Brown & Company, 1968), page 562.

2. John C. Maxwell, *Your Attitude: Key to Success* (San Bernardino, Calif.: Here's Life Publishers, Inc., 1984), page 66.

6 | Defining, Structuring, and Motivating

What is power? The "power of A over B," we are told, "is equal to maximum force which A can induce on B minus the maximum resisting force which B can mobilize in the opposite direction."
James MacGregor Burns,
"Leadership"

———

Leaders must be able to spot roadblocks and clear them.
John White,
"Excellence in Leadership"

———

There have been meetings of only a moment which have left impressions for life, for eternity. No one can understand that mysterious thing we call influence. . . . yet . . . every one of us continually exerts influence, either to heal, to bless, to leave marks of beauty; or to wound, to hurt, to poison, to stain other lives.
J.R. Miller,
"The Building of Character"

2 Samuel 8:1-18,
10:12

Organizing for leadership involves three concepts: defining, structuring, and motivating. Each of these concepts plays an important role in organizing life and career goals as well as personal and spiritual goals. Please pay close attention to each of these scriptural principles as you study 2 Samuel 8:1-18. See how often defining, structuring, and motivating surface as you examine this passage.

DEFINING

Unquestionably the first step in organizing is to define. Defining is far more important to the leader than to those who will be led. Unless the leader has clearly fixed his objectives in his own mind, aimlessness will characterize his career. Those who attempt to follow him may not immediately perceive that the leader's problem has to do with a lack of definition, but they will spot the aimlessness. Then their own reasons for following such meandering leadership will become unclear.

Your first attempts at defining are often not overt or visible. They are usually an inward attempt to sort out direction, velocity, and purpose. Defining is best done in writing. Direction, velocity, and purpose should all be stated in written form. They should always be accessible to you for review and amendment as you move toward your goals. These written definitions become the all-important boundary lines within which you play the game of leadership.

I believe the issue of defining includes four imperative elements: broadening, listening, condensing, and formulating.

The best definitions for living are written by those who have a broad range of experience and education. It only stands to reason that those who write great life definitions from a narrow world view will, of necessity, lead or define within a naive framework. Nothing is worse than trying to follow a leader whose life definitions are written from too narrow a framework.

Michael Thomas says that most would-be leaders lack a "liberal arts literacy" that provides the leader with "broader vision, a sense of history, [and] perspectives from literature and art."[1] One observer even remarked that graduate schools of business operate from too narrow a framework of understanding and thus do not provide the breadth of understanding out of which strong life defining can be done.[2] Another leadership luminary says that graduates of Stanford or Harvard often do not fare well in business circles because their degree work does not provide them with the flexibility to cope.[3]

Assuming that you have a broad education and experiential base, the next imperative of defining is to be a good listener. Definers are good listeners. Bennis and Nanus certainly agree with this:

> Therefore, the leader must be a superb listener, particularly to those advocating new or different images of the emerging reality. Many leaders establish both formal and informal channels of communication to gain access to these ideas. Most leaders also spend a substantial portion of their time interacting with advisers, consultants, other leaders, scholars, planners, and a wide variety of other people both inside and outside their own organizations in this search. Successful leaders, we have found, are *great askers*, and they do pay attention.[4]

The assumption that defining is primarily a matter of talking must be laid aside and replaced by an active willingness to listen.

The last two steps of the defining process, condensing and formulating, go together. Condensing simply means that you are able to extract and summarize important data from a broad experience and active listening. You cannot use all experience or all listening, so you must select from life experience; the wider the field, the more selective you must be. This data then becomes your own definition and premise.

Formulating, then, is taking these minute, extrapolated bits of data and writing conclusions that will serve as the boundaries referred to above.

STRUCTURING

Once you have completed the defining stage, structuring must begin. Structuring is the outlining and charting of your project or idea that enables you to know how your project is to be presented, enacted, and completed. Outlining is more complex than defining and requires your utmost discipline and thought. Sometimes the nature of your project may be too complex to allow you to be precise in implementing and detailing your outline. Even so, a general outline is still important. Structuring tells your followers that you as a leader are to be trusted because you can clearly explain the direction of the course you are taking.

MOTIVATING

Once defining and structuring are complete, you can begin the work of motivation. There are a number of ways to motivate, but affirmation, participation, and modeling are primary.

The first way to motivate others is by simple affirmation. When asked how he motivated basketball players, John Wooden answered, "I catch them doing something right."[5] There is little doubt that when you "catch people doing something right" and praise them for it, you employ affirmation in two ways. First, you affirm them simply by your praise. Second, you double that affirmation by praising them at the critical moment when they were doing right.

Next to affirmation, participation is an equally great motivator. One thing that must be said of Lee Iacocca's motivation at Chrysler was that the company employees had a sense of his participation with them. I don't know of any better way to illustrate this than to speak of it in terms of the player-coach relationship.

> Iacocca was equally impressive in the cultural realm. He had to change the cultural values from a "losers" to a "winners" feeling. . . . This Iacocca achieved, visibly and forcefully, by his frequent messages to the workers and, perhaps more important, by his own personal appearances in Chrysler ads to reinforce his internal messages.[6]

It means something to see the coach believe in the game enough to participate in the game.

Perhaps the most effective way to motivate is by modeling. Nothing motivates like a good example. Edmund Burke wrote: "Example is the school of mankind, and they will learn at no other."[7] Morton Hunt said his doctor prescribed a certain medicine for him that Hunt felt might be too dangerous. When Hunt confronted his physician by asking if the drug was dangerous, the doctor replied, "I take it myself." Morton said the words were easy motivators for him.[8]

As you study the life of King David, remember that David had these same motivational qualities in his leadership. They may not be as easy for you to track, but rest assured they were there. Perhaps as you begin this area of study, you could look at David's life in general (and this passage in particular) and see if you can pick out aspects of leadership that seem to indicate that David was good at defining, structuring, and motivating. As you do this, you need to develop your own understanding of these aspects of leadership.

Questions for Discussion
1. LEADERSHIP IS PROCEEDING WITH A SIMPLE PLAN
Perhaps you should look at a Bible study map as we attempt to understand 2 Samuel 8:1-3. David's course of military conquest followed a very simple plan; he subdued his enemies by encircling his own country with those he had conquered. He moved in a counterclockwise fashion until, instead of being surrounded by active enemies, he was surrounded by subjugated peoples.
  a. Most good books on leadership say it is important to keep your plan for succeeding simple. David seemed to move from subduing the weaker nations (Phylistia) to the stronger ones (Syria). What does this say about the simplicity of his plan? What does it say about the psychology of his motivation?
  b. Think about your structuring process for meeting your goals. In what ways do you work simply? In what

ways do you tend to build complex systems that im-
prison even your own thinking?

c. What evidences are there in these verses that David
knew how to prioritize?

d. Do you know how to prioritize? How can you increase
this skill?

e. Should a plan, even a simple plan, be flexible? Why or
why not?

2. LEADERSHIP IS STRUCTURING FOR STABILITY

After the conquests, David garrisoned, or occupied,
enemy territory with troops loyal to himself (2 Samuel
8:6,14).

a. How is David's military practice different from that of
Saul before him?

b. Why is stabilizing intermediate goals important to
success?

c. What is the relationship of structuring to management? Of management to stability?

d. How long do you think David's conquest would have
been effective without his garrisons?

e. What might be the consequences of setting goals
without thinking about what you will do once your
goals are achieved?

f. Once you have won a primary plateau of success, how
soon should you move on to your secondary goals?

g. Is it possible to switch goals too capriciously to be able
to complete the imperative process of defining, struc-

turing, and motivating? What stabilization tactics might allow for slower, better judgment in the process?

3. LEADERSHIP IS JUDGMENT AND JUSTICE IN ADMINISTRATING

In 2 Samuel 8:15, we see that David, like other good leaders, was just and wise in his administration.

a. Many leaders can motivate but not properly administrate. Do you think this was true of David? Explain why or why not.

b. All the world is interested in a fair shake. What does the word *fair* mean in administration?

c. Can every ambiguous expectation a leader has be clearly spelled out so the followers know exactly what is expected of them? Explain.

d. The word *judgment* in verse 15 (KJV) implies good judgment. What would a leader with good judgment do about the use of time?

e. How would a good leader regard the limitations and feelings of those he leads?

f. What are some ways a good leader could remember that all people are different and special, and that everyone wants to be thought of and treated in a special way?

4. LEADERSHIP IS DELEGATING TASKS AND RESPONSIBILITY

In chapter seven of this study, we will consider the issue of delegating in more detail. For now, read 2 Samuel 8:16-18 and consider how David delegated various tasks.

a. Do you think David also delegated the authority to accomplish the tasks? Why did he handle it this way? (Many leaders want to delegate work but grant no real authority. Such delegation is based on insecurity and mistrust.)

b. In what ways is it possible or impossible for a leader to be a good organizer or manager without taking the issue of delegation seriously?

c. In what ways must a good leader understand people and the individual differences between them in order to be an effective delegator?

d. In what ways are delegating and resource management the same?

e. As a leader, describe your ability to delegate a job and completely trust the person assigned to accomplish it.

f. If you have had a job in which you felt your boss didn't trust you to accomplish what he asked you to do, write down the lessons you learned about leadership.

5. LEADERSHIP IS MOTIVATING BY EXAMPLE

a. Second Samuel 10:12 is a statement made by Joab, one of David's followers. Would you say that David motivated his followers by modeling how to remain stable in the pursuit of all goals, regardless of the crisis?

b. Do you think David's leadership style is an example of a leader who concentrated on goals rather than on the problems that sometimes obscure the goals? Why do you think this?

c. At what times in your life have you allowed your goals to be clouded by personal problems that deflected your vision?

d. Do you think David motivated others by being their buddy or by being their boss? Which type of motivation do you think is best?

e. What role do a leader's ethics play in motivation?

NOTES

1. Michael M. Thomas, "Businessmen's Shortcomings," *New York Times*, August 21, 1980, page D2, cited by Thomas J. Peters & Robert H. Waterman, *In Search of Excellence* (New York: Harper & Row, 1982), page 35.

2. Peters & Waterman, *In Search of Excellence*, page 35.

3. Peters & Waterman, *In Search of Excellence*, page 35.

4. Warren Bennis & Burt Nanus, *Leaders: The Strategies for Taking Charge* (New York: Harper & Row, 1985), page 96.

5. Cited in David L. McKenna, *Renewing Our Ministry* (Waco, Tex.: Word, Inc., 1986), page 139.

6. Bennis & Nanus, *Leaders*, page 145.

7. Cited in Alan Loy McGinnis, *Bringing Out the Best in People* (Minneapolis: Augsburg Publishing House, 1985), page 92.

8. Cited in McGinnis, *Bringing Out the Best in People*, page 93.

7 The Politics of Grace

Assumption of personal authority, marked self-confidence and political skill, the diminution of legislative and party opposition, personal and dramatic links with the people, the enhancement of executive function and responsibility, the exploitation of emergency powers—these are the qualities of executive leadership.
James MacGregor Burns,
"Leadership"

—

The power to persuade is the power to bargain.
Richard Neustadt,
"Presidential Power"

—

Someone says: "The only thing that walks back from the tomb with the mourners and refuses to be buried, is character." This is true. What a man is, survives him. It never can be buried.
J.R. Miller,
"The Building of Character"

2 Samuel 9:1-13

Politics is a word of contempt for people in the church. Church politics seems more ungodly than civil politics. "We must keep politics out of the church," say the offended.

Mark this!

In every organization, the leader is somewhat of a politician who learns how to motivate various people to do the right job. The leader must recruit people—making commitments, side-deals, complimenting, remonstrating, and sometimes bargaining—to get things done. In 2 Samuel 9, David demonstrated the political overtones of his leadership. Do not think David unspiritual for behaving as he does to Mephibosheth. The truth is, he is being especially effective.

I remember being terribly incensed some years ago when a good pastor friend suggested that every successful pastor was a politician. I determined that even if he spoke the truth, I would rather not succeed than use politics in any aspect of my ministry. I actually held some resentment toward him until I later read a similar statement in a book by a pastor-writer who I had always admired. Gradually I felt I was living free of the whole issue. But in moments of honest thought, I realized that politics need not be a dirty word when used in the context of ministry.

Our distaste for the word *politics* is set in concrete in the aftermath of national scandals like Watergate, the Iranian arms deal, or those that have rocked television evangelism from time to time. The truth of the matter is, *politics* isn't just a dirty word; it really means to use our sphere of interpersonal relationships in ways that enable us to accomplish the most. *Politics* is defined in the dictionary as the "art and science of government . . . the art of influencing policy or winning control." Only a secondary meaning of *politics* that emphasizes competition between groups or individuals for power and leadership.

Of course, the very suggestion that pastors or churches ought to be caught in power struggles is unworthy of the Cross. But let us remember that the basic word *politics* is related to the word *polite*, which means any action that is marked by courtesy, consideration, or correct social usage. I would like us to focus on politics in the sense of courtesy and correct social usage. Jesus certainly did not encourage power struggles in the church. He did say that kindness and courtesy were the laws of His Kingdom. He said that the Christian was to be wise, knowing his world, but harmless as far as the desire for power or control was concerned (Matthew 10:16). He even went so far as to compliment an unjust steward by saying that the children of this world are wiser in their generation than the children of light (Luke 16:8). In these verses, is Jesus condoning a "Watergate" in the church? Of course not! But He is saying that a thorough knowledge of this world is important and the kind of diplomacy and courtesy employed in the world might often benefit the Kingdom of God.

Practically, this means you are not free as a Christian to compete for power in this world or in the church for your own use. But you are free to seek to promote God's Kingdom in the hearts of men and to establish the Church of Jesus in this world. If by courtesy, deference, or kindness you cause enemies to love each other or the power-prone to join the cause of Christ, then politics is good. The key to the whole issue is: are you using deference, courtesy, and public relations to get others to accede power to you for your sake, or are you using these things to create a new and wider sphere of influence for God in this world?

It is wise to remember that Jesus was victimized by civil politics at His trial. Although He had all power, He succumbed to the political machinery of the Romans, Pharisees, Sadducees, and Zealots; His life was crushed. Much harm is done in the church because we forget the corrupting nature of power. It is easy to want to control others for our own advantage. We easily degenerate to "tit for tat," battling politics with politics. However, the Cross says we are not here to control, but to widen God's influence in the world.

In this passage, David of Israel used his old friendship with Jonathan to promote goodwill between warring political camps in Israel. David knew what he was doing and used deference and courtesy in a splendid way. The result of his kindness to Jonathan's crippled son produced a new harmony and better relationships in Israel. May we learn to use such courtesy and practice the politics of grace.

Questions for Discussion
1. **THE POLITICS OF LEADERSHIP: Using Special Interest to Moderate Ideological Conflict and Bring the Greatest Number of People into Workable Unity**
   In 2 Samuel 2-4, David and his supporters killed all of the house of Saul to keep any claimants to that dynasty from rising in revolt. Doubtless there were deep grudges throughout the kingdom because of this purge. So in 2 Samuel 9:1, we see David the leader looking for new ways to bring the diehards who still were loyal to the house of Saul into orbit with his own goals.
   a. Does David do something illegal in hopes of reclaiming the loyalty of some of the house of Saul?
   b. Can you think of a time in a religious group when special-interest action was taken to bring separate factions into workable unity?
   c. Do you agree or disagree with the statement, "The pastor should never play politics"? Why?
   d. At the conference recorded in Acts 15, a statement was issued that Christians should not eat meat offered to pagan idols. Paul, however, seemed to reverse this decision in 1 Corinthians 8:4-8. Why do you think Paul seemed to make a rule for the Corinthian Christians that did not apply to Christians in Jerusalem?
   e. Do you consider Paul's solution to be a special-interest solution for those who served Christ in a predominantly pagan culture? Explain your reasoning.

2. THE POLITICS OF LEADERSHIP: Using Special Interest for Patronage

Patronage means to use special interest to gain support. Jesus' final words in the parable of the dishonest steward (Luke 16:1-9) are, "Use worldly wealth to gain friends for yourselves"! Jesus' statement is almost a dictionary definition of patronage.

a. Is it good to use patronage to solidly lock people into an organization or cause? Why or why not?

b. What experiences have you had with people whose use of patronage was self-serving, but who tried to appear selfless?

c. In what ways do you think David did or did not exercise good leadership in his patronage of Mephibosheth? (See 2 Samuel 9:3-7.) Is the phrase "buttering him up" a fair way to describe David's patronage?

d. In what ways might those who are patronized take advantage of their special treatment to gain their own control of a company or church?

3. THE POLITICS OF LEADERSHIP: The Allocation of Resources to Keep the Maximum Number of People Happy

With so many people in the house of Mephibosheth and Ziba (2 Samuel 9:10), it must have taken quite a bit of the king's resources to feed and clothe them. A real leader can sometimes see, however, that money must be spent to change discord into harmony. David seemed to act with this thought in mind.

a. Can you remember a time when you saw your pastor (or other church leaders) take special-interest action to bring a sense of harmony and peace to the whole church? Describe what happened.
b. How would you harmonize such special-interest action with the beatitude, "Blessed are the peacemakers" (Matthew 5:9)?
c. Describe a time in your life when a church leader had to give you special consideration. Have you had to return such consideration to someone else?
d. Is it possible that politics within the church could be endorsed by God for building unity? Give an example.

4. THE POLITICS OF LEADERSHIP: Image Building and Title Conferment
Second Samuel 4:4 describes how Mephibosheth became lame. In 2 Samuel 9:3,13, Mephibosheth's lameness is mentioned at least three times.
a. Is David culpable here of political compassion?
b. Would most handicapped people today resent receiving special interest because they were handicapped? What support do you have for your answer?
c. While David's treatment of Mephibosheth might have built David's image in 1000 BC, would it do so today? Explain your answer.
d. In what ways might Mephibosheth's new status have given him and/or David a new esteem with others?
e. Can you think of situations in which title conferment

or other positive image building has helped develop a great church? Describe what happened.

5. THE POLITICS OF LEADERSHIP: Helping Subordinates Move Up the Staircase

One of the joys of special-interest action is watching people find new levels of status.

a. Do people always welcome the new status of others? Can you think of anyone who might have resented Mephibosheth's promotion?

b. How would you relate the statement, "It is amazing what could be done in this world if no one cared who got the credit" to David's situation?

c. Do you think David befriended Mephibosheth because of love for Mephibosheth's father, or because of the glory he anticipated from his expression of political compassion?

d. What steps could you take to help others achieve personal satisfaction?

e. In what ways might these actions demonstrate your potential for leadership?

8 Leadership: The Importance of Delegation and the Team Spirit

In the best-selling book, *In Search of Excellence*, the authors point out that the best-run companies in America invariably have employees who share the pride of the corporate name.
David L. McKenna,
"Renewing Our Ministry"

Speak for yourself, John.
Henry Wadsworth Longfellow,
"The Courtship of Miles Standish"

Now this is the law of the jungle,
It's as old and as true as the sky,
And the wolf that shall keep it may prosper
And the wolf that shall break it must die.

As the creeper that girdles the tree trunk,
The truth runneth forward and back,
For the strength of the pack is the wolf,
And the strength of the wolf is the pack.
Rudyard Kipling,
"The Law of the Jungle"

2 Samuel 23:8-17   G ood leaders never give their leadership away, but they share the visibility and responsibility of leading. One of the outstanding Bible passages on this concept is in Exodus 18:21-22, where Jethro (Moses' father-in-law) noticed Moses' extreme fatigue and suggested that Moses not try to do all of the counseling in the camp of Israel by himself. Jethro's solution was to suggest that Moses delegate some of his counseling load to others.

Paul Tournier noticed that much of our contemporary world is caught in the ravages of what he calls "universal fatigue."[1] I wonder if a part of this universal fatigue is not traceable to the fact that many leaders have never quite learned how to share the burden of their leadership with others.

So often a company consists of a few hassled, harried leaders and a great many followers. Generally, the followers have not been challenged to participate in the workload of those who lead, and no great leader can live long in this condition. Followers must be made to believe they are a part of the team. They must be made to participate with the leader in the work the team has to do. Such participation will level out both the "busyness" at the top and the lacka-daisical attitude at the bottom. Bennis and Nanus have addressed the various problems that exist in the realm of job commitment.

> Fewer than 1 out of every 4 jobholders said that they are currently working at full potential.
> One half said they do not put effort into their job over and above what is required to hold onto it.
> The overwhelming majority, 75 percent, said that they could be significantly more effective than they presently are.
> Close to 6 out of 10 Americans on the job believe that they "do not work as hard as they used to." (This may or may not be true, but it's their perception.)[2]

You can never achieve great leadership without effective delegation. By delegation, you will increase the job commitment of others by spreading your task effectively over a broader base. As others feel more responsible for your work, they begin to care about the outcome. But in order to build a true team spirit, you must delegate accountability and glory as well as responsibility. Because of our human selfishness, it is clear that accountability and glory are far harder to delegate than responsibility.

You can never arrive at a real plateau of leadership by insisting that others do your work while you take the glory. Even a leader must be a team player. Real leaders make followers accountable for the task they have been delegated. When the task is finished, any fault that has accrued will belong to your followers. So, on the other hand, will be any accompanying glory. It is also wise to remember that your followers' ability to accept the pain of their failure or glory of their success is directly related to the role model you supply. If you bear your responsibility in an accountable way, those to whom you have delegated a task will also feel the same way.

David's wonderful ability to delegate is seen in 2 Samuel 23:8-17. The fact that the men mentioned here are all worthy of honor in David's monarchy shows that David knew how to share a task—and when the work was done, the glory. The mention of these mighty men of valor suggests that David was not the only person who was allowed to wear such titles in ancient Israel. David's generous spirit is the hallmark of a true leader who can share the load and be a team player.

In studying the life of David in chronological sequence, it is hard to know where to put 2 Samuel 23. It makes some sense to place the events of 2 Samuel 23 near the end of King David's long reign. In that context, the passage portrays the old king reflecting over his youth and recalling the various team members that helped him subdue the land. However, the same events are also recorded in 1 Chronicles 11:11-47, where they are placed after the capturing of the citadel (Jerusalem). I have decided to locate this important event chronologically after 2 Samuel 5, which deals with the young king as he occupies his new capital for the first time.

Regardless of where we place the events of this passage chronologically, its message is one of leadership and team spirit. Only the deeds of three of the thirty knights mentioned are spelled out, but we may be sure that all were equally important. As David reflects on their deeds, he names each man, and we learn the importance of a loyal team and the leader's ability to delegate the issues of influence to trusted subordinates.

Questions for Discussion
1. DAVID'S TEAM AND THE TASKS HE DELEGATED
   Adino the Eznite (2 Samuel 23:8, KJV). What had he done to further David's military campaign? Do you think this superhuman feat was accomplished out of his loyalty to human leadership or divine leadership?

   Eleazar, the son of Dodo (2 Samuel 23:9-10, KJV). He fought "until his hand was weary, and his hand clave unto the sword," or until he couldn't let go of it. His support of David, the leader, would have to be called steadfast. What qualities make followers go to such committed extent for their leaders?

   Shammah, the son of Agee (2 Samuel 23:11-12). Of these three knights, Shammah is the most curious. He defended a lentil (or bean) field. One cannot help but remember all of those who are spoken of as "not being worth a hill of beans!" Yet this outworn cliché becomes his glory.
   a. Great followers are faithful even in lowly responsibilities like protecting a bean field. This bean field is immortalized in Scripture as a lesson of faithfulness. But how much trust should a leader extend? How

often should a leader delegate assignments and check back on the trustee?

b. Shammah is celebrated by the king for his execution of his assignment—his name even appears in Scripture. Should a leader always take time to celebrate the achievement of loyal subordinates? Why or why not?

2. THE TEAM'S DEPENDABILITY

If 2 Samuel 23:15-17 is placed in proper chronological arrangement, this event obviously occurred at a time in David's life when Bethlehem (his hometown) was under Philistine occupation. What David asked seems capricious, but not before the fact. After his men brought him water from his hometown, David was ashamed of the danger he caused his trusted team. As he poured out the water before God, he surely confessed his folly.

a. When a leader delegates a project to his subordinates that he later feels was inane, should he publicly ask forgiveness? How could asking forgiveness weaken or strengthen his image in the eyes of those on his team?

b. How does a great leader expose his vulnerable, human side to those who have spent a part of their life working on a bad idea that he assigned?

c. How do people respond to visible weakness in a leader?

d. How does perceived weakness affect future leadership?

NOTES
1. Cited in Robert Banks, *The Tyranny of Time* (Downers Grove, Ill.: InterVarsity Press, 1983), page 40.
2. Warren Bennis & Burt Nanus, *Leaders*, page 7, citing Daniel Yankelovich & Associates, *Work and Human Values* (New York: Public Agenda Foundation, 1983), pages 6-7.

9 Leadership and the Abuse of Power

We know that a common characteristic of all mental patients is their powerlessness.
Rollo May,
"Power and Innocence"

——

People used to ask me what I wanted to be when I grew up, and I was shrewd enough to fashion my answer according to what I thought they wanted to hear. . . . However, in my own heart of hearts, I had my own private fantasy. . . . *I wanted to be president of the world!*
John R. Claypool,
"The Preaching Event"

——

All weakness tends to corrupt, and impotence corrupts absolutely.
Edgar A. Friedenberg

2 Samuel 11:1-15   Charles Reich, nearly two decades ago, wrote that it was not so much the misuse of power that was evil, but its very existence. Although his statement seems harsh, almost every abuse of power grows out of someone's perverted affair with himself.

The path to abusive power is easily traceable. It begins simply in our need for appreciation. From there the path winds upward to self-esteem, which—when it takes itself too seriously—moves toward arrogance. Arrogance often disparages others and leads to abusive power.

The roots of abusive power are often found in men and women who were once victimized by power. For this reason Rollo May, in his book *Power and Innocence*, says that it is not always power that corrupts; indeed, powerlessness may be the corrupter. Powerlessness may be a prison for the unconquered spirit—a prison from which cell mates dream of being free and, once free, create the same abusive cells of powerlessness in which they force others to live. Sigmund Freud noticed that most boys had psychological vendettas against their fathers. In early life these vendettas can lead them to begin vying with their fathers for power. Such vendettas produce powerful men who wield great, and sometimes abusive, power. James MacGregor Burns, in his Pulitzer Prize winning book, *Leadership*, says that Adolph Hitler, for instance, is rumored to have been born with an undescended testicle. Such a child in a male-oriented world may struggle to achieve power in order to compensate for his deformity.[1]

When examining David's role in history, it is futile to speak of his character formation in such ordinary terms as an oppressive father or physical deformity. The truth is, God seems to have placed David in a leadership role in order to forge a disorganized, tribal government into a nation. David clearly was not crushed by feelings of powerlessness, but he must have had such feelings from time to time.

Any condition of powerlessness, such as not being esteemed in childhood, may cause a person to strive extra hard to become an influential adult. Comedian Rodney

Dangerfield has popularized the idea of how the lack of outer esteem can cripple us. "I get no respect," he laments for everyone who feels the full impact of powerlessness.

Did David ever feel that he "got no respect"? In the case of David's anointing (1 Samuel 16), his father Jesse appeared to esteem him least of all his sons. David's menial job of shepherding while his more gallant brothers were warriors might suggest—if only by reason of his youth—that he was not esteemed to be competent enough to go to war. If so, David's powerlessness may have become a springboard into the center of attention and national leadership.

We cannot assume that David tried to show the world that he "got no respect" and thus became a *Forbes, Inc.* super-achiever. Nor did David exhibit, after his rise to the throne, very many abuses of power. The growth of personal authority can be a platform for effective leadership, but it can also be the threshold of exploitation and power abuse. Most of David's life is marked by the former quality, but in 2 Samuel 11, we see the latter.

Leaders whom James MacGregor Burns would call "moral leaders" are those whose motivation is to produce changes in the world that will be of real value to both the leader and those he leads.[2] However, abusive power fails to see the followers and makes decisions in which the welfare of others is not a real concern. In such a "pro-me" use of others, the universe becomes a "you-niverse" in which others exist solely for the power abuser.

I suspect that most power-mad leaders never define themselves that way. They operate with the same mind-set as when they saw others as worthy of existing for their own reasons. Their erosion to the abusive use of power was so gradual that they may not have seen it. On their way up the ladder of control, they may well have served those they led; they were moral leaders. But once they gained the pinnacle of control, the power they had once been willing to share became their sole province.

The pinnacle of position that power-mad leaders occupy often causes people around them to admire, and even envy, them. Admiration often feeds our cancerous self-esteem until we, in "Mohammed Ali" fashion, can say with little embarrassment that we really are the greatest! Arrogance, when well fed, begins to believe that the world owes it whatever it can seize.

This was apparently David's philosophy in 2 Samuel 11. How did it develop? While we cannot know exactly when and where David's sinful abuse of power began, we can see that by 2 Samuel 11 the king's heart had turned from servant leadership to scandalous power.

Servant leadership is the all-important checkpoint that bridles demonic power. As long as we follow Christ, we are safe! It is impossible to live out Christian servanthood and wield the mace of abusive power. He who tries to rule from the throne of Christ is a usurper, and not a servant. David learned this truth as a consequence of his evil deeds, but in Psalm 51 we see that he learned the beauty of the words that close the Lord's Prayer: "*Thine* is the Kingdom and the *power. . . .*"

We are servants as long as we remember what Jesus said to Pilate: "You would have no power over me if it were not given to you from above" (John 19:11). We need to repeat this truth in every area of leadership to ensure that we truly are servant leaders.

Questions for Discussion
1. **POWER ABUSE EVIDENCE #1: Giving Up All Disciplines Common to "Underlings"**
"At the time when kings go off to war," David didn't go (2 Samuel 11:1). No reason is offered for his failure to go with the army. He did not seem to be ill or incapacitated. War is dangerous, but David was no coward. War is hard, but David had once thrived on what was difficult. It appears as though David had excused himself from war solely on the basis that he was king and could do as he wished. His self-excusing reason may have been, "Even though it is customary, I owe this to me."
a. We have already said that power abuse is rooted in selfishness. What steps might David have taken to ensure that the disciplines that had forged him into a moral force would not decay?

b. What steps can you take to ensure that you do not "cop out" of your responsibility and become indulgent?

c. David must have viewed dying as the duty of "underlings" while he had the right to enjoy the more exalted status of being king! What does this say about the dignity of all men?

d. Is such a degenerative view of human dignity common in all power abuse? Cite some examples.

2. POWER ABUSE EVIDENCE #2: Thinking That Others Owe Me Whatever Use I Can Make of Them

In 2 Samuel 11:2-3, Bathsheba and her husband became objects for David's personal use. Power abuse is characterized by using others. It is well said that we ought to love people and use things, not use people and love things!

Some pastors and religious workers have found ladders to personal success within church or parachurch organizations. While on the rise to power, by using those they were called to serve, some have continually quoted Philippians 2, which speaks of Christ who humbled Himself and became nothing. They do not always realize what they are doing and when confronted, they deny it in favor of the more humble image of themselves they prefer.

a. Did David continue writing psalms during the time he used Bathsheba and plotted her husband's death? Is it possible that he was faithful in his attendance at temple worship during this time of power-mongering?

b. Is it possible to have a devotional life of sorts and take advantage of people at the same time? If so, how?

c. What do you think of the concept of "double think" (the mental gymnastics by which we simultaneously accept two contradictory values in our mind)?

d. In what ways could "double think" apply to David's walk with God and his affair with Bathsheba?

3. POWER ABUSE EVIDENCE #3: Trying to Fix Things Up Rather Than Make Things Right

This evidence of power abuse shows the art of manipulating circumstances without moral conscience. David's sin in 2 Samuel 11:6 was that he didn't start with his sin. Instead, he engineered things to a favorable end rather than doing the hard moral and spiritual work of getting right with God.

a. How often do you find yourself making a mess of your circumstances, yet thinking in terms of how to fix things up rather than to make things right? This tendency is common with power abusers.

b. In the next chapter we will see that David ultimately gets things right with God, but his first attempts were to fix things up. The truth is, we don't usually think of asking God how to make things right while we are trying to fix them up. Do you think David thought of "getting right with God" at this stage? What leads you to think this?

c. Do you see evidence that David was too insensitive to God to even understand the phrase "power abuse"?

d. What spiritual steps might you take to ensure that you confront your personal sins rather than adjust your circumstances?

e. In what instances might "getting right" be the same as "fixing up"?

4. POWER ABUSE EVIDENCE #4: Closing My Mind to Every Suggestion That I Am Out of God's Will

If King David had been sensitive to walking with God, he probably would have heard a rebuke in Uriah's suggestion (2 Samuel 11:11) that the men of Israel were dying in the field and therefore he would not live in selfish ease.

a. At which times in your life have you been so involved in selfish indulgence that you were blind to the signposts that God put in your way to call you to Himself?

b. How do we keep our eyes open to the lessons that God sends our way?

c. Is verse 11 evidence that power blinds us to God's rebuke? What other incidents in this story can you see that God used to nudge David toward repentance?

d. Have you pursued pleasure while others were in great pain or lived under great hardship? Evaluate those times.

e. Do you think the American church "lives it up" while Christian brothers in other cultures are dying? If so, in what ways?

f. In what ways might apathy be an evidence of the abuse of power?

5. **POWER ABUSE EVIDENCE #5: Thinking That People in My Way Are Expendable**
In 2 Samuel 11:14, Uriah's refusal to return home for even one night, which would have made Bathsheba's illicit pregnancy appear to be the natural result of fidelity, became an embarrassment to the king. So David took steps to eliminate Uriah so that he could marry Uriah's widow and "legitimize" the pregnancy.
   a. Could David have arranged this tidy elimination of Uriah if he had really considered Uriah's worth to God? Explain.
   b. At what times has your personal agenda caused you to forget how much God loved your antagonist?
   c. In what ways did Uriah's Gentile status contribute to David's tendency to see him as expendable?
   d. What hidden prejudices in your life cause you to see your characteristics as more esteemed than others?
   e. When you see someone whose power tends to destroy others, how can you confront that person with the dignity of every man?

NOTES
1. James MacGregor Burns, *Leadership* (New York: Harper & Row, 1979), pages 61-62.
2. Burns, *Leadership*, page 41.

10 Can a Leader Survive a Visible Mistake?

I wish that there were some wonderful place
    Called the Land of Beginning Again,
Where all our mistakes and all our heartaches,
    And all of our poor selfish grief
Could be dropped like a shabby old coat at the door
    And never put on again.
Louise Fletcher Tarkington,
"The Land of Beginning Again"

I bargained with Life for a penny,
And Life would pay no more,
However I begged at evening
When I counted my scanty store.

For Life is a just employer,
He gives you what you ask,
But once you have set the wages,
Why, you must bear the task.

I worked for a menial's hire,
Only to learn, dismayed,
That any wage I had asked of Life,
Life would have paid.
Jessie B. Rittenhouse,
"My Wage"

I'm too big to cry and it hurts too much to laugh.
An American presidential candidate,
upon losing the election

2 Samuel 11:16-26,
12:1-7; Psalm
51:4,12-14

No great life has ever been lived without pain and error. As king of Israel, David had celebrated a progression of victories and national successes. The acclaim these successes brought may have caused him to take liberties with his strict sense of right and wrong. For when we receive too much acclaim it is easy to believe that we have a right to behave without moral controls. Perhaps David's stardom had brought him to this point.

David's survival of his affair with Bathsheba shows that great leaders can indeed survive a mistake. I believe survival is best achieved when three factors enter into play: openness, forgiveness of others, and a recognition that we are all in process.

Openness is an almost imperative quality in a leader's life. Those who live in openness survive mistakes the best. Actually, openness is an admirable quality if you lead for a good number of years (or even all of your life) and never make a visible mistake.

Crises such as Watergate or the Iranian arms scandal make it clear that almost all of us are more tolerant of mistakes admitted than mistakes denied. In King David's case, he did, for a while, try to cover up his affair and its crimes as evidenced by his murder of Uriah and duplicity with Nathan the prophet. But what is admirable is that once he is discovered, David's openness declares that he is not above reproach; even kings can be guilty of great sin. Psalm 51 is a public acknowledgement of King David's sin and need for repentance.

A second quality a leader must seek as gold is a spirit of forgiveness toward followers who, from time to time, will sin. When Jesus said, "In everything, do to others what you would have them do to you" (Matthew 7:12), He was not merely stating a nice principle of life. He was stating a key truth that applies to every arena of leadership. A follower you treat with charity is far more prone to forgive you when you are caught in a storm of contempt.

Jesus told a parable about a steward who was forgiven a great debt, but in the wake of his forgiveness became hard and unforgiving. To cry, "Pay back what you owe me!"

(Matthew 18:28) is hardly defensible after a great debt has been forgiven. In His model prayer, Jesus taught us to pray, "Forgive us our debts as we also have forgiven our debtors" (Matthew 6:12). Such a prayer lies at the heart of surviving a mistake. If your followers remember your charity in a moment of great need, they will lay away the gift of mercy for your future need.

There is one final quality to develop if you genuinely wish to set yourself up to be forgiven for your mistakes. You must communicate to people that you are a real human being and, like all the world around you, are a person in process. Process people are much easier to forgive when they are caught in error than those who try to project that they are complete and full of wisdom. The right to grow is an important right.

You can establish the idea that you are a person in process by doing a very simple thing: Let those around you see you change your mind from time to time. Let others see you do things differently than you did yesterday.

One of Gandhi's disciples once confronted him in desperation: "Gandhiji, I don't understand you. How can you say one thing last week, and something quite different this week?"

"Ah," Gandhi replied, "because I have learned something since last week."[1]

David had lived with his best warriors for a long time. I like to believe that David's close proximity to his men allowed them to see him as a person in process and that his close living with these men had avoided the remoteness that often keeps leaders from being open to the world. Doubtless David had a forgiving spirit as well. Without these qualities, the Bathsheba affair might have destroyed him. With these qualities he was able to live many more productive years as the leader of his nation.

It is rare for an indulgent soul to grant itself only one liberty. Usually one granted liberty becomes the foundation of future license. After having sent the army rather than leading it, David became easy prey to sexual indulgence (2 Samuel 11:2-5).

After Bathsheba became pregnant, the king tried to

protect himself from scandal. First he tried the cover-up approach. Then, under pressure, he openly dealt with the problem.

Questions for Discussion
1. THE COVER-UP APPROACH
The cover-up approach (2 Samuel 11:6-17) is almost totally ego-defensive and is based on the idea that "people will think less of me if they really know what I am or what I have done." However, the truth is that people can usually accept weaknesses more easily than they can accept hypocrisy.

David's hypocrisy falls primarily into two areas: an attempt to fool his friend Uriah (2 Samuel 11:8-13) and an attempt to deceive the nation (2 Samuel 11:14-17).

a. Twice David attempted to get Uriah to sleep with his wife, Bathsheba, so David's child would appear to be Uriah's own. What rationale do you think David used to justify his deception?

b. Uriah was a Gentile. Why is it sometimes easier to trivialize people who are the brunt of our prejudices or grudges?

c. Is it possible that David felt the end of his action would justify the means? Would it have done so? Does it ever?

d. As David tried to get his friend drunk, he demeaned his friendship with Uriah. Do you set aside spiritual integrity by taking advantage of other people, even in simple ways?

e. David wrote psalms of praise. How is it possible to live a life abundant with praise and worship and yet practice a life of scheming?

f. Do you think that David, by this time in his rapidly degenerating walk with God, may have stopped praising God altogether? What does this tell you about the role of praise and worship in your life?

g. The second, more elaborate act of scheming proves that David went national with his deception. In the first part of 2 Samuel 11, David wanted Uriah and Bathsheba to continue as a married couple and have a family. Later it became clear that David decided to take Uriah's wife, thus deceiving the whole nation. In this act, the king's cover-up became complex. David's crime was a slur on Uriah's faithfulness. His cover-up involved Joab and the army. This decision amounted to murder, so the consequences were indeed serious. Do you think the king was aware that this complicated cover-up was entirely ego-defensive? Why do you think this?

h. How powerful is your own need to preserve your image before friends and associates?

i. What steps might you take to test why you act as you sometimes do? How can you devise checkpoints that indicate you are living a life of self-surrender and not self-protection?

2. THE OPENNESS APPROACH (PSALM 51:4,12-14)

In David's case, the openness approach turned out to be an induced openness. No doubt, 2 Samuel 12:1-7 reveals why David became so open: Nathan's parable forced the deceptive king to openly acknowledge that he had been guilty of immorality and murder. Psalm 51 is the painful evidence that the king is opening his life before God and the world.

a. David acknowledges in Psalm 51:4 that his primary sin was not against Bathsheba, Uriah, or even Israel, but God. Is it possible to have any real relationship with God while we see our sins and their consequences only in terms of the human beings we have wronged? Explain your answer.

b. In this case, David's sins were pointed out by the prophet. How can you train yourself to see that your "horizontal" sins against others may really be "vertical" sins against God?

c. David's plea for a restored joy in verse 12 prompts this question: How can we have any real joy while we are hypocritical and fail to live in complete openness before God?

d. Remember, God knows that we have sinned, so repentance isn't telling God what He does not know; it is a willingness to open our lives to God's cleansing. What do you think is the real relationship between a clean life and God's forgiveness?

e. What is a good procedure for recovering lost joy?

f. After his cleansing, David promised to teach transgressors and praise God (verses 13-14). Can we effectively work with those who have no relationship with God while our own relationship with God is damaged? Why or why not?

g. How is praise affected when we harbor unconfessed sins?

h. Is the kind of openness we have been discussing possible on any basis other than a cleansed life? If so, on what basis?

NOTE

1. Larry Collins & Dominique Lapierre, *Freedom at Midnight* (New York: Simon & Schuster, 1975), page 106.

11 Leadership: Coping with Difficult People

Power is always interpersonal.
Rollo May,
"Power and Innocence"

———

Baptista: Why then, thou canst not break her to the lute?
Hortensio: Why no, for she hath broke the lute to me.
William Shakespeare,
"The Taming of the Shrew"

———

I beseech Euodias, and beseech Syntyche, that they be of the same mind in the Lord.
The Apostle Paul,
"Epistle to the Philippians"

2 Samuel 21:11-14

I f you would lead, know this: Coping with difficult people is a must! Beware of the sincerity myth—the error that teaches that criticism is not customary and that you will be able to avoid all criticism if you are sincere and utterly truthful.

Every great leader has learned that problem people are customary and must be dealt with every day. So let us begin this study by defining them. Difficult people are those who stand between you and the realization of your objectives. They usually are a deterrent to the earliest possible achievement of your objectives.

It is helpful to remember that a heart-cry to be loved often lurks behind the obstinacy of many problem people. So sometimes the best way to eliminate a critic is to make him or her your friend. Assuming this has been tried, however, your problem people may have to be met on another basis.

One difficult type of person you must learn to deal with is the Chronic Arrogant type. Chronic arrogant persons are usually covering for a bad inferiority problem, and their arrogance is merely their way of coping. Their chief characteristic is an apparent feeling that their ideas are the only ones that matter. Chronic arrogant types are not always brutal in relationships, but they are strong willed. Socrates believed that all of humanity could be divided into two types: the wise who know they are fools, and the fools who believe themselves to be wise. Chronic arrogant persons would fall into the latter category.

The best way to deal with chronic arrogant persons who are not convinced of the value of humility or modesty is to wait until life's hard circumstances come. I have found that the parable of the lion helps me wait:

A terrifying lion once met a cowardly monkey in the jungle. The lion pounced on the poor shaking monkey and asked, as he breathed damnation in the monkey's face, "Who is the king of this jungle?"

The monkey was terror-stricken and quickly acceded, "You are, O King!"

The lion let him go.

Next, the lion met an elephant. He roared out insults to the elephant, asking him the same question. The elephant was not so easily intimidated. With his trunk he picked up the lion and slammed him against a tree fifty feet away. The lion walked away and said very meekly, "Just because you don't know the answer is no reason to get rough."

People who play rough usually meet someone even rougher. The encounter often tames their heavy-handedness and makes them endurable.

As Christians, we are taught that "cheek turning" is the proper way to handle aggression. When dealing with a chronic arrogant person, I recommend turning the other cheek, but being sure he does not become a steamroller, smashing those who are in the way of his personal agenda. The solution lies in keeping your chin firm while you turn the other cheek.

Another difficult type of person with whom leaders must cope is the type I call the congenitally belligerent— one who has been upset since the womb. Congenitally belligerent people differ from the chronic arrogant in that they are aggressive and verbally abusive. Rough circumstances do not slow down the congenitally belligerent as they do the chronic arrogant. In fact, congenitally belligerent persons love a fight and thrive on conflict.

It is unlikely that your most conscientious efforts will bring even a momentary sweetness of spirit to such people. David Seamands relates how someone very close to one such person remarked: "Joyce, you certainly are an even-tempered person—you're always mad."[1] Seamands also tells about a congenitally belligerent person who was described as having colitis. Overhearing the remark about colitis, a little boy asked, "Who's she been colliding with now?"[2]

Congenitally belligerent people are always upset. They are always colliding with someone. In any organization, they will be colliding with the leader. So to be an effective leader, you must take the collisions head-on, assuring these difficult individuals that they will gain nothing through belligerence. You must handle their belligerence with a firmness that conveys that you are a person, too.

Norm Evans tells about a football lineman who had a problem with an opposing lineman. He took the problem to his coach saying, "He keeps pulling my helmet over my eyes. What should I do?"

The coach wisely answered, "Don't let him do it!"[3]

Congenitally belligerent people must be stopped! Another motivator refers to congenitally belligerent people as Sherman tanks. They must be stopped. They must not be allowed to roll over the leader or any followers who are doing their best to serve the leader in a productive way.

I call a third type of difficult person the Non-negotiator. These persons confront your leadership with a unique challenge: silence. Non-negotiators usually remain quiet in an attempt to keep away from all organizational transaction, but their silence is intended to diminish the opportunity for others to share. By refusing all negotiation, they are inaccessible and block progress by their silence. Non-negotiators must be confronted in as frank a way as possible and be made to disseminate what they know would advance the project.

Just as silence can be used by non-negotiators, so can whining. Whining is a ploy used consistently by many problem people to avoid negotiation. Whiners use whining to bring some kind of commiseration in their direction. Thus whining non-negotiators become powerful persons. These do not whine until their grievance is answered, or sympathized with; they whine because it gives them an edge in controlling their business relationships.

Remember, as a leader you usually cannot make these people happy by acceding to their demands. Their real demand has nothing to do with your conciliation. Their selfish need for recognition and attention is the problem.

The difficulty in dealing with this type of person is that they seem to be in pain. Their aim is to make you feel especially heartless if you confront them. But make no mistake about it; manipulating your feelings is their intentional ploy. They must not be allowed to delay the objectives of the team.

There are plenty of other types of difficult people. Consider for a moment the Blockbuster type—the congenitally belligerent who has gone so far as to steamroll over others' ideas and opinions. Here the firmest leadership must be employed, for this type of person can be desperately hard to stop. Blockbusters can be so dangerous to group morale that they may have to be fired to keep their "march to the sea" from destroying everyone and everything. It is better to lose the blockbuster than to watch one person destroy all corporate teamwork and the corporate dream.

One of the difficult types most irritating to me is one I call the Nitpicker. Nitpickers chisel and snipe at good ideas by focusing on molehills at the expense of mountains. Their minor objections can drag projects to a grinding halt. If you suggest that a nitpicker is majoring on minors, he or she may collapse in self-pity or launch into a belittling tirade. The nitpicker must be constantly challenged to focus on things that really matter.

The difficult Wheedler who whines, cries, and groans to have his or her way is similar to the non-negotiator, but is more communicative. Wheedlers will negotiate, but will use a grieving tone the moment you begin to suggest solutions that may force them to bend a little. They can be so unpleasant that others will let them have their way rather than risk the unpleasantness of listening to them lose.

Wheedlers are aware of the psychological power of their demeanor. Seeing others retreat often hastens toward negative aggression. As a leader, you can challenge a wheedler by asking, "Can you state your feelings about this more positively?" or "Aren't you happy today?" or "Must you be so melodramatic?" or "Let's have the facts only. We'll decide if we want to feel as negatively about this as you do."

The Nay-Sayer is a difficult person who greets every great idea by saying, "Yes, but it won't work for this reason." This type is easy to spot because the word *but* always immediately follows the word *yes*. Nay-sayers can point out aspects of an issue or project that are likely to go wrong, so it is good to listen to them. Unfortunately, their heavy negativity is often a blockade for everything right. Therefore it is best to

use them for private advice or place them in a less conspic-
uous role where their negativity will have little influence on
great decisions. This type of person must be asked to state
feelings without prejudicing others about the outcome.

The successful Christian leader must not only handle
all of these difficult types, but must do it with the realization
that even the most difficult people are loved by God and
have a right to dignity. So the key issue in coping with
difficult people is to handle them without belittling them
before others. Love is the key ingredient even in the direst
circumstances in which some sort of rebuke, which should
be as private as possible, is necessary.

As a leader you must determine if a person who is
causing trouble is really a difficult person or merely trying
to express a real difficulty with the issue at hand. Difficult
people and people with difficulties are two different things.
So you must study and understand both.

Leaders have to build their worlds with the materials at
hand. Although it is difficult to place 2 Samuel 21 chronologically, it makes one point clear: every leader must live
with the *status quo*. David's kingdom and bright dreams were
surrounded by life circumstances from a previous regime.
Throughout David's reign, these pre-existing conditions
continually surfaced, causing difficulty. As a leader, David
had to deal not only with future issues, but with the ghosts of
troubles that plagued his world before he began to lead it.

David's difficult people were the Gibeonites. Consider
the six issues that came into play in David's circumstance
when coping with the difficult people in your life.

Questions for Discussion
1. CAN YOU FIND OUT WHY GOD SENDS THE
DIFFICULT PERSON INTO YOUR LIFE?
We don't know exactly why the Gibeonites and the
three-year famine came at the same time in David's life
(2 Samuel 21:1). David assumed that the famine was the
result of Saul's crimes against the Gibeonites. (The mas-
sacre referred to in 2 Samuel 21:1-2 is not mentioned
elsewhere in the Bible, so we cannot know its real
nature.)

a. David assumed that problem people came along to show why bad things happen to good people. How do you view problem people? Are they a chance to learn about personal weaknesses, or do you allow problem people to exist without trying to read any divine meaning into their effect on your life?

b. The enemies of Saul became the enemies of David. How can a leader ease the criticism he or she inherits from the existing leadership structure?

2. WHICH OLD ENEMIES SHOULD BE SOUGHT FOR RECONCILIATION?

a. Undoubtedly, David had many enemies. Why do you think he singled out the Gibeonites (2 Samuel 21:2) and decided that their request was most urgent?

b. In singling out your critics, how do you establish the pecking order to determine which of your enemies should be heard first?

3. HOW FAR SHOULD YOU GO TO SATISFY THE COMPLAINTS OF AN OLD ENEMY?

a. Assuming that problem people have a real grievance, how far should you be willing to go to correct the grievance?

b. Does the issue of how far back in time the grievance occurred affect the consideration you give? If so, in what way?

c. It is likely that the complaints of the Gibeonites infiltrated the citizens of Israel (2 Samuel 21:3). When should the continual murmuring of problem people be rebuked? When should it be placated?

d. If it is impossible to make everyone happy, what criteria would you use to discover which people can be placated and which ones cannot?

4. WHEN PROBLEM PEOPLE BECOME TOO SEVERE, ARE THEY WORTHY OF YOUR EAR?

I have found, through many years of ministry, that my critics often seek vengeance for old ills in ways that cannot be toned down. In 2 Samuel 21:6, the Gibeonites were crying "crucify."

a. Do you think David handled their outcry in a stern way? How might he have handled it differently?

b. David obviously tried to silence the Gibeonites' outrage and keep them within the framework of Israel's government. Was this wise?

c. When might it be best for severe critics to leave an organization rather than allow their severity to affect others?

d. How would a good leader go about discerning whether critics should be appeased or asked to leave?

5. ARE POLITICAL SOLUTIONS PERMISSIBLE IN DEALING WITH PROBLEM PEOPLE?

In 2 Samuel 21:8, the Gibeonites are politically appeased when David delivers Saul's heirs for execution. In 2 Samuel 21:13, Rizpah, Saul's wife (concubine), is politically appeased after watching her hanged sons rot in the hot harvest sun for a summer.

a. Was this appeasement a good device to keep everybody happy?

b. How do you think God felt about the way David solved this problem?

6. IS IT IMPORTANT TO LIVE WITH OLD ENEMIES CONGENIALLY?

a. We all make enemies from time to time. Do you think David's exaltation of his old enemies (2 Samuel 21:14) is out of genuine love, or merely an attempt to create goodwill among dissidents?

b. Can you live with old enemies, even if they never change and become your friends?

c. Suggest some biblical ways to deal with old animosities.

NOTES

1. David A. Seamands, *Healing of Memories* (Wheaton, Ill.: Victor Books, 1985), page 73.

2. Seamands, *Healing of Memories*, page 91.

3. Steve Brown, *No More Mr. Nice Guy* (unpublished manuscript), page 93.

12 Leadership: Adjustment in Management Style

I will not be the man I was.
Ebenezer Scrooge,
"A Christmas Carol"

———

Be not conformed to this world, but be ye transformed by the renewing of your minds.
The Apostle Paul,
"Epistle to the Romans"

———

"Look at me, Tom, I'm the last of my kind.
Take charge of your life, Pal, you must change to find
All living is changing, begin with your mind."
The Dinosaur,
"Tommy and the Dinosaur"

2 Samuel 21:15-22   Every leader is at the mercy of his or her own flexibility. If you cannot adjust as your organization grows, you will soon be obsolete. My experience in helping a church grow from 10 to 2,500 members has taught me that I am the single greatest enemy to our continued forward progress. At one plateau of membership size, I must relate to the church administration in one way. At a larger size, I must vary my style of administration. Leadership adjustment is imperative in the long haul.

Change is a big word! Change will be readily seen as a great quality in your life by those who honor tolerance and understanding, but it will only be seen as fickleness if you have been intolerant toward others. David McKenna wrote, in *The Psychology of Jesus,*

> People grow and change by stops, starts, jumps, and fallbacks along a trend line. Ross Mooney, a psychologist friend, once compared human development to the exercise of walking. A body is in balance when standing still. In order to walk, however, imbalance must be risked as one foot moves forward. In that state of disequilibrium, the body has a natural drive for stability; so the trailing foot is signaled forward and balance is regained.[1]

Still, most leaders needlessly greet change reluctantly. Arnold Lazarus and Allen Fay describe six myths of change:

Myth 1: If you have knowledge and understanding—in other words, if you know why you are the way you are, or why you do the things you do, or why you feel the way you feel—then you will change.

Myth 2: If you don't know the reasons behind your behavior, you won't change.

Myth 3: It takes a long time to change. After all, you have had problems for a long time.

Myth 4: If you change fairly quickly, it is superficial and it won't last.

Myth 5: It is frequently impossible to change. "This

is the way I am, and this is the way I'll always be."
Myth 6: If you are middle-aged or older, it is too late to
      change.[2]

Adjustment in leadership style keeps leadership contemporary. Adjustment in leadership style means that the
leader has already agreed that the direction of his leadership is not on course and, rather than continuing to lead in
the wrong direction, he is making a correction in mid-course.
      In management style, most leaders realize that this is
their basic way of relationship which, if changed, wars
against comfort. This kind of change immediately says to all
concerned, "The way we have felt about each other and
reacted to each other may have to change for the benefit of
the common task we serve."
      I serve as pastor in one of the faster growing, large
denominations. Still, most churches in our denomination
are not growing. In fact, seventy-nine percent of our
churches are either static or in decline. What great deterrent keeps churches from growing? I believe a lack of
growth can be attributed to a failure on the part of individual pastors or leaders to adjust their management styles.
      One church growth expert says most churches will not
grow to the size where they will require more than two
people on staff because most pastors cannot share the glory
of congregational veneration with more than one other
person. This factor of management is so locked in with the
pastor's psychological need for esteem that pastors often
seem unable to change enough to enable their congrega-
tions to grow.
      I began as pastor in the parish I serve some twenty
years ago. The management of the church from a very small
one to a very large one means that I have had to change my
management style continually. As our congregation grew
from one size to the next, I had to change in order to relate
to more members. I had to learn to delegate more of my
workload to others who serve with me. I am grateful to many
laymen who helped me grow in my ability to change.
      David of Bethlehem must have gone through the same
kinds of management changes as he grew from a renegade,

guerilla fighter to a real monarch. As we examine his management style, let's pay particular attention to his ways of relating to his followers as Jerusalem changed from a small Jebusite city to the capital of government.

Every change in the organization means that a leader must adjust and manage in a different way than before the change occurred. In 2 Samuel 21:15-22, it becomes clear (assuming this passage is in its correct chronological position) that Israel had grown to the place where David could not govern exactly as he did when he was a mountain chieftain fleeing from Saul. Four principles of management style that every leader must consider if his leadership is to grow and expand stand out as noteworthy.

Questions for Discussion
1. OVERCOMING FATIGUE IN A GROWING ORGANIZATION
A lot of attention is being given to *burn out* these days. Simply defined, *burn out* results from psychological overload and is a fatigued withdrawal from responsibility.

In 2 Samuel 21:15 (KJV), David "waxed faint," which means he suffered from fatigue. Overwhelming fatigue can affect every leader.

a. What are some common, practical steps you can take to eliminate fatigue from your life of leadership?

b. How often is your fatigue the result of tired muscles, and how often is it the result of a lack of excitement, goals, or direction?

2. SOURCES OF COUNSEL IN A GROWING ORGANIZATION

David's men gave him some advice in 2 Samuel 21:17 which he seemed to accept.

a. In small organizations, great ideas can come from almost anyone, but in large organizations, great ideas tend to flow from the top down. What can be done to resist this trend?

b. Smart leaders listen to their constituency. What steps could pastors and board members take to hear from members of the congregation?

c. Which kind of leader, the affirming leader or the demanding leader, is most likely to pick up new ideas from others? Why?

d. How can a leader discover if others see him as a listener?

e. In what ways could channels for sharing advice be set up in a company or church?

3. SHARING THE GIANTS TO BE KILLED

Ishbi-Benob needed to be dispatched (just as Goliath had been earlier in David's life), but David did not need to do it personally. Giants are sometimes the last thing for a leader to give up. This is probably because countering giants is the fun part of leadership. The worst thing about giving up giants is the loss of joy and celebration once they are slain.

Remember that early in David's life the great cry had been, "Saul has slain his thousands and David his ten thousands" (1 Samuel 18:7). There David learned how wonderful it is to slay a giant and get the credit. Because of the incident in 2 Samuel 21:16-20, the people are doubtless crying in the streets, "David has slain his thousands but Abishai his ten thousands."

a. In your opinion, how much of David's reluctance to quit slaying giants was due to the accolades of the people and how much to his desire to follow the will of God?

b. Do you think David sent Abishai a "thank you" card for taking care of Ishbi-Benob? Why or why not? Does David seem like the kind of man who could celebrate the great deeds of others?

c. How do you think the cliché, "It is easier to weep with those who weep than to rejoice with those who rejoice" applies here?

d. How might a leader live and enjoy life through the exploits and triumphs of his subordinates?

e. Is it possible to assign a task to someone, celebrate its completion, and still retain the respect of those you lead? Did David retain his leadership by assigning this task to another?

4. THE IMPORTANCE OF THE FAMILY TO THE LEADER OF A GROWING ORGANIZATION (2 Samuel 21:21)

David's nephew was also a giant-killer.

a. How important is the family of an effective leader?

b. In what ways should an effective leader cultivate family relationships that sustain and nourish his or her life?

c. David's wives are not mentioned here (in ancient Israel women may have been seen as less important than in our contemporary world), but how might an effective leader's home life prepare him or her to be more effective?

d. What difference does it make when a family nourishes the life of a leader?

NOTES

1. David McKenna, *The Psychology of Jesus* (Waco, Tex.: Word, Inc., 1977), page 59.

2. Arnold Lazarus and Allen Fay, *I Can If I Want To* (New York: Warner, 1975), pages 16-17.

13 The Leader: Bridge Builder to the Future

I have seen the future, it is much like the present only
longer.
Kellogg Albran,
"The Profit"

——

Nkrumah lacked the imagination and skill to develop a
country. He was a revolutionary without a plan—a visionary, but not a builder.
David Apter

——

Man will not be able to excuse himself at the last judgment,
saying to God, "You overwhelmed me with the future
when I was only capable of living in the present."
Author unknown,
"The Cloud of Unknowing and The Book of Privy Counseling"

1 Kings 1:32-35,
2:1-11

Death eliminates the future. David died, like all of us will, on the threshold of other people's futures. Yet he was optimistic on his deathbed.

John Maxwell tells of a conversation that occurred on an elevator. The elevator was crowded and one passenger seemed irritated by another's cheerfulness.

"What are you so happy about?" he snapped.

"Well, sir, I ain't never lived this day before!"[1]

Such optimism marks the real leader. Every great leader is a futurist. He considers what today's decisions mean in tomorrow's world. At age eighty-three, Frank Lloyd Wright was asked which of his works he would select as his most important. The answer was easy: "My next one!"[2] No leader is satisfied with yesterday's performance. The best is yet to be done.

I have always liked the story of the old professor who was reading Plato. Someone asked him, "Why are you reading Plato at your age?" He answered saucily, "Why, to improve my mind, of course." Futuristic replies mark those who see leadership as significant.

It seems that most of mankind has set out at a furious speed to go nowhere. But real leaders are always setting out to go somewhere. The leader sees that the journey can never be completed in the moment, for everything worthwhile ends in the future.

The future can, of course, be scary. There seems to be a kind of mercy in our heavenly Father that He does not let us see very far down the road He wants us to travel. Lee Iacocca expressed this view of the future beautifully:

> It's a good thing God doesn't let you look a year or two into the future, or you might be surely tempted to shoot yourself. But He's a charitable Lord: He only lets you see one day at a time. When times get tough, there's no choice except to take a deep breath, carry on, and do the best you can.[3]

While God's mercy does not let us see very far down the road we must travel, He is also the wonderful God who lets us know the future is on the way. The thought of the future fuels every leader with zeal, for true leaders do not glory long in the past or present. The Apostle Paul comments on what is probably the futuristic mind-set of leaders:

> But one thing I do: Forgetting what is behind and straining toward what is ahead, I press on toward the goal to win the prize for which God has called me heavenward in Christ Jesus. (Philippians 3:13-14)

The press of every leader is the mark of the high calling of God—a mark that is yet to be achieved—a crown that is yet to be worn.

In essence, this idea of the future comprises all that is brightest in human hope. Viktor Frankl, who spent years in a concentration camp, noticed that those who believed in tomorrow best survived the day. Those who believed that tomorrow would never come were those who could not survive:

> The prisoner who had lost his faith in the future—his future—was doomed. With his loss of belief in the future, he also lost his spiritual hold; he let himself decline and become subject to mental and physical decay.[4]

The future is glory! Indeed, the future is survival.

I have known many successful men and women. Without exception, all of them had a healthy view of the future that led each of them to a spirit of unbridled optimism. To believe in the future is to be optimistic.

Many successful people have adopted little slogans by which they ride out the rough times. Like Little Orphan Annie, they believe that "the sun will come out tomorrow." Or, under the heavy press of seeming failure, they will cry, "This, too, shall pass!" I have known others who quoted, "When you walk through a storm hold your head up high," or another slogan of hope.

In the midst of crushing despair, the Christian leader also relies on the sufficiency of the Bible's great truth. In

1 John 3:2 we read, "Dear friends, now we are children of God, and what we will be has not yet been made known. But we know that when he appears, we shall be like him, for we shall see him as he is." The motivation for hanging onto the future is hidden in God's continuing faithfulness. After all, "Jesus Christ is the same yesterday and today and forever" (Hebrews 13:8).

But the leader is not only future-oriented, he is future-connected. *Thoroughly Modern Millie* gloried in the fact that everything today was thoroughly modern, making everything yesterday seem slow. And that is a bit true. The leader realizes that no matter how glorious the moment is, it will look rather quaint in a short period of time.

So the key is not to take the moment so seriously that it cannot be released. The present connects the past and future; the real leader sees no real break between the two. The future is not a discontinuous "yet"; it is firmly attached to the moment. Since the present and future cannot be separated, they must be considered as one. Leaders who operate from this concept are never surprised that the future gets here suddenly, because they know it is on the way. So the real leader owns tomorrow because he never forgets how firmly it is attached to today.

At the time of his death, David of Israel was aware that even in death he could not act irresponsibly, for the future was already on the way. He knew that at the very moment of his death, tomorrow—with all of its demands—would be firmly attached to the moments he could not survive. Thus, as he died, he acted exactly as he had all along. He could not die and merely be dead; even his death had to be a step toward the future, which he could not inhabit, but had to influence. Such is the magnificent, futuristic mentality of leadership.

The end of life should be the bridge to all that follows. The passing of a monarch always presupposes the question, "Who will be the next king?" On his deathbed, David saw a quarreling, struggling set of princes, each of whom were the egoist imprint of himself. It must have been chilling for David to view the ambition of his quarreling sons. Since their potential struggles could set the nation to civil war,

David took some practical steps to ensure a secure future. Let's examine those steps.

Questions for Discussion
1. UNDERSTANDING WHAT THE FUTURE NEEDS
I do not believe that David picked out his favorite son to succeed him in 1 Kings 1:32-35. Instead he asked which of his sons would best cope with the needs of a growing nation.
a. In light of the glory that was to mark Solomon's reign, was David's choice a great choice? Explain your answer.
b. In what ways were Solomon's wisdom and ability in architecture an improvement upon David's capabilities?
c. If David's contributions to the establishment of Israel were primarily military, how would you categorize Solomon's contributions?
d. Do great leaders have to be like their forebearers? Why or why not?
e. What were the differences between David and Solomon? Were the differences good?
f. David's poems and Solomon's proverbs seem to indicate that both of them were immensely creative writers. Do creative administrators tend to have other kinds of creative talent? Cite an example.
g. Following Solomon's reign, the nation fell into civil struggle and divided into two nations. Do you think Solomon took the same care David did to lay the rails to the future? Explain your answer.
h. Kings find it easier to appoint their predecessors than some other leaders do. What practical steps can corporate or church leaders take to influence the choice of the right team for the future?
i. How much leeway should pastors and other church administrators be given to select their own church officers and staff members?
j. Can the future of an organization be over-administrated and therefore perpetuate the same evils that were in the regime that nominated the future?

What type of honest analysis would ensure that only the best parts of the past are saved for the future?

2. THE COVENANT WITH GOD

In 1 Kings 2:1-4, we see that David rehearsed the importance of Solomon governing in league with God. Every Christian leader is but an extension of God's sovereignty.

a. When considering the future of an organization, how can the faith of future leaders be challenged to face the future with God?

b. In 1 Kings 2:2 (KJV), David said to Solomon, "Play the man!" This seems like macho advice. What do you think David meant?

c. At what times did David "play the man"?

d. At what times did Solomon "play the man"?

e. In 1 Kings 2:3, David said that Solomon needed to keep four things if he were to walk in the future ways of God. What do you think he meant by each of these phrases: God's statutes; God's commandments; God's judgments; God's testimonies?

f. In 1 Kings 2:4 we read God's promise of dynasty to David. The best way to ensure the future of God's rule on the earth is to let Him reign in the present. We continually face the risk that the future will be discontinuous with the past. The monsters that devour us don't come from our past, but from the misty "not yet." The primary requirement of the future, therefore, is faith. How did the dying king tell the future king to live?

g. How is devotion to God related to success in leadership?

h. Did David's prediction for Solomon's heir to the throne come true? What does this indicate about Solomon's covenant with God?

3. ELIMINATING THE PROBLEMS OF THE PAST TO KEEP THEM FROM BECOMING FUTURE PROBLEMS

a. In 1 Kings 2:6,9, David singles out Joab and Shimei to be dealt with. Every good leader gives the future the benefit of all he knows. Why did David distrust Joab and Shimei?

b. Is it safe to assume that old enemies will never change? Should one attempt to reclaim an old enemy or eliminate all possibility of his danger to the future? Explain your answer.

NOTES

1. John C. Maxwell, *Your Attitude: Key to Success* (San Bernardino, Calif.: Here's Life Publishers, Inc., 1984), page 25.
2. Maxwell, *Your Attitude*, page 25.
3. Lee Iacocca, *Iacocca: An Autobiography*, with William Novak (New York: Bantam Books, 1984), page 141.
4. Viktor E. Frankl, *Man's Search for Meaning* (New York: Simon & Schuster, 1985), page 85.

14 A Review of Leadership Principles

Miss Duggan, will you send someone in here who can distinguish right from wrong?
A cartoon,
"The New Yorker"

—

Undeniably, some people in this world walk around with chalk on their toes because they stand too close to lines in life that must not be crossed.
Richard J. Ferris,
Chairman, Allegis Corporation

Now that you are at the end of this study of David's life, you may need to view it as the beginning of your life as a leader. Consider the thirteen concepts we've examined. Make a list of the key truths that have most impacted your life. But before you list them, spend some time in prayer. Decide how you currently arrive at your self-image and what you might do to improve the place you give God in evaluating all your strengths and weaknesses.

Along with self-image, reconsider Proverbs 29:18 and the issue of vision. There is no question about it: the men and women who have vision have more meaning in life than those who do not. There is no such thing as a leader without vision. David was able to forge a monarchy out of the ashes of his vanquished predecessor. His success was largely a matter of seeing life's possibilities and formulating steps for achieving them. The issue is clear: a leader must see the finished state of what he or she wants to create before it has a chance of being.

Good leaders want God to be involved in the process of making decisions. Second Samuel 6:1-15 rehearses the anatomy of a good decision. Part of the agony faced by all Christian decision makers is trying to make a decision when there seems to be no clear word from God. We have not specifically studied King Saul in this Bible study, but consider this: 1 Samuel 28 shows Saul caught in a time that called for decision, yet he had no clear word from the Lord on how to make the decision. By consulting the witch of Endor, Saul abandoned godly faith at a time when God was silent. Every leader has sometimes sought God's help and found God silent. But a worthy leader still trusts and decides in faith, even when God seems elusive.

Learning to share the business and burden of organization is absolutely mandatory. In chapters five and eleven, we saw the leader in roles of adjustment and delegation. Recall again the deeds of the three specific knights celebrated in 2 Samuel 23:8-12. What were their deeds? How did they carry out their tasks? Now consider David's other top thirty knights. Their names are recorded but not their deeds; could specific deeds be called forth in the lives of each of them that would define their sphere of influence as it had been assigned?

In building a team, it is important that each team member see himself or herself as strategic in the whole task of the organization. Honor yourself with a great gift: learn to communicate dignity, self-importance, and organizational importance to each team player. Always remember that each team member has need for self-fulfillment.

One of the key areas of leadership that is hardest to remember is that God loves all the problem people in your life as much as He loves you. If you remember this, it may occasionally call to mind the possibility that others may have viewed you as a problem person in their lives.

Along with these problem people, we have also considered power, networking, and adjustment in management style. My prayer is that in my own life I will do as I've encouraged you to do. I want to seek from Scripture the reinforcement of the principles conveyed through these chapters.

Study the Bible as you study leadership. You will then add good morality to your leadership recipe. You will also find the Bible to be a wellspring of quietude that will provide the depth of soul you need to stabilize the ups and downs of leadership. The more the wisdom of Scripture pervades your views, the more those around you will trust you. And trust is the keen edge of the blade with which you sculpt your life. Psalm 119:11 says that God's Word is a lamp; read it and lead with light.

Books for Further Study

Banks, Robert, *The Tyranny of Time* (Downers Grove, Ill.: InterVarsity Press, 1983).

Bennis, Warren & Nanus, Burt, *Leaders: The Strategies for Taking Charge* (New York: Harper & Row, 1985).

Blanchard, Kenneth & Johnson, Spencer, *The One Minute Manager* (New York: William Morrow and Co., 1982).

Brown, W. Steven, *13 Fatal Errors Managers Make* (Old Tappan, N.J.: Fleming H. Revell Company, 1985).

Buck, Lee, *Tapping Your Secret Source of Power*, with Dick Schneider (Old Tappan, N.J.: Fleming H. Revell Company, 1985).

Burns, James MacGregor, *Leadership* (New York: Harper & Row, 1979).

Engstrom, Ted W., *The Pursuit of Excellence*, forward by Senator Mark Hatfield (Grand Rapids: Zondervan Publishing House, 1982).

Hoekema, Anthony A., *The Christian Looks at Himself* (Grand Rapids: William B. Eerdmans Publishing Company, 1975).

Iacocca, Lee, *Iacocca: An Autobiography*, with William Novak (New York: Bantam Books, 1984).

Levitt, Theodore, *The Marketing Imagination* (New York: The Free Press, Macmillan, Inc. 1983).

Maslow, Abraham H., *Toward a Psychology of Being* (New York: Van Nostrand Reinhold, 1986).

Maxwell, John C., *Your Attitude: Key to Success* (San Bernardino, Calif.: Here's Life Publishers, Inc., 1984).

McCormack, Mark H., *What They Don't Teach You at Harvard Business School* (New York: Bantam Books, 1984).

McGinnis, Alan Loy, *Bringing Out the Best in People* (Minneapolis: Augsburg Publishing House, 1985).

Miller, J.R., *The Building of Character* (Chattanooga, Tenn.: AMG Publishers, 1980).

Osborne, Cecil G., *The Art of Becoming a Whole Person* (Waco, Tex.: Word, Inc., 1978).

Peters, Thomas J. & Waterman, Robert H., *In Search of Excellence* (New York: Harper & Row, 1982).

Schaller, Lyle E., *The Decision-Makers* (Nashville: Abingdon Press, 1974).

Smith, Fred, *You and Your Network* (Waco, Tex.: Word, Inc., 1984).

Waitley, Denis, *The Double Win* (Old Tappan, N.J.: Fleming H. Revell Company, 1985).

Besides books of the type that appear in this bibliography, you will want to acquire many other leadership resources. Be open to such leadership sources as audio and video tape series. Cassettes are a good use of automobile time as you work at self-management. *Sound Ideas* are books on tape from Simon & Schuster. *Fast Track* is a similar series of management book tapes by Macmillan. You may also want to give special attention to all or any of the tapes in the Nightingale-Conant library of leadership and management.